SUBSTANCE

An insider's view of success and failure in government

Nick Raynsford

First published in Great Britain in 2016 by

Policy Press
University of Bristol
1-9 Old Park Hill
Bristol BS2 8BB
UK
t: +44 (0)117 954 5940
e: pp-info@bristol.ac.uk
www.policypress.co.uk

North American office:
Policy Press
c/o The University of Chicago Press
1427 East 60th Street
Chicago, IL 60637, USA
t: +1 773 702 7700
f: +1 773-702-9756
e:sales@press.uchicago.edu
www.press.uchicago.edu

British Library Cataloguing in Publication Data
A catalogue record for this book is available from the British Library.

Library of Congress Cataloging-in-Publication Data
A catalog record for this book has been requested.

ISBN 978-1-4473-3192-6 paperback
ISBN 978-1-4473-3194-0 ePub
ISBN 978-1-4473-3195-7 Mobi

Contents

List of abbreviations

ACAS	Advisory, Conciliation and Arbitration Service
ADP	Approved Development Programme
AGMA	Association of Greater Manchester Authorities
ALMO	arm's length management organisation
BRE	Building Research Establishment
CFOA	Chief Fire Officers Association
CPA	Comprehensive Performance Assessment
DCLG	Department for Communities and Local Government
DETR	Department for the Environment, Transport and the Regions
DTLR	Department for Transport, Local Government and the Regions
FBU	Fire Brigades Union
FRA	Fire and Rescue Authority
GLA	Greater London Authority
GLC	Greater London Council
HIP	Home Information Pack
HMOs	houses in multiple occupation
IDeA	Improvement and Development Agency
IT	information technology
LDDC	London Docklands Development Corporation
LFEPA	London Fire and Emergency Planning Authority
LGA	Local Government Authority
MP	Member of Parliament
NHS	National Health Service
NJC	National Joint Council
ODA	Olympic Delivery Authority
ODPM	Office of the Deputy Prime Minister
Ofsted	Office for Standards in Education
OGM	Office of Government Commerce

List of abbreviations

PM	Prime Minister
RDA	Regional Development Agency
RMB	Regional Management Board
SHAC	Shelter Housing Aid Centre
SNP	Scottish Nationalist Party
SPAD	special adviser
TfL	Transport for London
UK	United Kingdom
UKIP	United Kingdom Independence Party

Preface

The book explores the way in which government in the UK seeks to translate policy into practice. It draws heavily on my own experience but is not, I hasten to add, a politician's diary. There are already too many, of which only a few shine out. Among those the diaries of my former colleague Chris Mullin deserve special mention.[1] I could not and do not hope to emulate Chris's acute observation of the personal foibles of those engaged in the political process, which makes his volumes such compulsive reading. Instead I seek to explore how and why particular policies find their way into the political arena, and what are the main factors contributing to their success or failure. In doing so I highlight some of the weaknesses (as well as the strengths) of the administrative and parliamentary systems that we operate currently, and suggest changes that would, in my view, help to improve the quality and effectiveness of government in the UK. I firmly believe that this is fundamental if we are to address and overcome the widespread public disenchantment with politics and politicians, which represents a seriously corrosive threat to our democracy. Because of the particular responsibilities I have held, the main illustrations I have used come disproportionately from England, but I hope and believe that a number of the conclusions that emerge are relevant to the whole of the UK, and indeed may have wider relevance.

This book could not have been written without the help of many others. It spans a period of more than 40 years, during which time I have worked with and discussed the themes covered in the following pages with a huge number of people, far too many for all to be acknowledged. To those who will recognise some of the events described and be aware of their own contribution, but whose names do not appear in the following pages, I can only offer my sincere apologies. Limitations on space have inevitably restricted the number of people whose work, advice, guidance and support are openly acknowledged. All of these have contributed actively to the preparation of this book, sharing their memory and interpretation of events, offering views and critiques of my analyses, correcting errors and suggesting improvements in the text. I have been very struck, and touched, by the willingness of former colleagues to open their memories and archives and let me have the benefit of their experience, years and, in some cases, decades after the events. They include: Mike Ash, Keith Berryman, Michael Burton, Max Caller, Jessica Crowe, Alun Evans, Paul Everall, Charlie (Lord) Falconer, Don (Lord) Foster, Michael Gahagan, Jane Groom, Joan Hammell, Keith Hill, Bob (Lord) Kerslake, Sir Ken Knight, David Lock, Anthony Mayer, John O'Brien, Jules Pipe, Steve Quartermain, Tony Redpath, Martin Simmons, Lee Shostak, Tony Travers, Steve Wilcox, Katy Willison and Philip Wood. Needless to say, they have no responsibility for any errors that may have crept into the text, nor for the opinions expressed, which are mine alone.

Over the years I have been helped and supported by several brilliant PAs, and work partners, and I would in particular like to acknowledge the input of Oonagh O'Toole, Gill Morris, Alison Seabeck and Kate Myronidis, to all of whom I owe a particular debt of gratitude for helping to make possible many of the positive outcomes described in this book.

I am grateful to Melanie Dawes, Permanent Secretary at the Department for Communities and Local Government, for making appropriate files in the Department's archive available to me, and her staff, who could not have been more helpful in identifying and assembling the relevant papers. Sight of these has been hugely important to me in checking the accuracy of my own memories. They too have no responsibility for my opinions and my interpretation of events.

I have been lucky to have stumbled on a truly supportive publisher, and wish to record my grateful thanks to Alison Shaw and her team at Policy Press for making this author's experience of writing his first book such an enjoyable and largely problem-free experience.

Thanks are also due to the Chartered Institute for Housing, the Town and Country Planning Association, and the Institute

Substance not spin

for Public Policy Research for permission to reproduce tables and graphs that originally appeared in their publications.

Very little that is described in this book would have been possible if I had not had the support of members of the Labour Party who selected me as parliamentary candidate, first in Fulham and subsequently in Greenwich and Woolwich, and the electorate in both constituencies who gave me the opportunity to serve as their Member of Parliament (once in the case of Fulham, five times in the case of Greenwich and Woolwich). I remain, as I hope is clear from the following pages, a passionate believer in good government and social justice delivered through the democratic process. I am deeply grateful for having had the opportunity to try to give effect to those beliefs in the time I served in Parliament, and so am also grateful to Tony Blair and John Prescott for giving me the opportunity to serve as a minister in, respectively, their governments and departments.

Few people can navigate the choppy waters of public life without a supportive home and family, and I would in conclusion like to record my huge debt to Alison Seabeck (now Raynsford), my wife, who has been a tower of strength, given me constant encouragement and shown remarkable patience in the course of the past year when I have been putting together the material for this book. I also owe a deep debt of gratitude to Anne Raynsford, my first wife, who lived through and supported me through so many of the events described in the following pages. To them and our three daughters, Catherine, Laura and Helen, who are a huge inspiration, I dedicate this book.

ONE

The problem

We live in an age when, to put it mildly, public confidence in our democratic institutions is at a low ebb. Not just in Britain, but across a swathe of countries in the developed and developing world, there is growing evidence of cynicism about the political process, the trustworthiness of politicians, the effectiveness and integrity of public institutions and the ability of governments to deliver their promises. Of course this is not an entirely new phenomenon. The history of the past two centuries is littered with examples of democratic governments failing to meet the hopes and aspirations of their electorate. Indeed, even before the emergence of recognisably modern democratic models, those engaged in the processes of politics and government did not always enjoy a good reputation. King Lear's advice to the blinded Gloucester:

> Get thee glass eyes and like a scurvy politician seem
> to see the things thou dost not,[1]

could not give a clearer indication of Shakespeare's unflattering view of those engaged in early 17th-century politics. A degree of scepticism about the motivation of our rulers, coupled with an inclination to mock their foibles and lampoon their behaviour, has long been recognised as a healthy sign of a free society and a necessary antidote to the tendency towards self-importance among those in positions of authority. When it is not possible to laugh at a political leader without fearing imprisonment or, worse, a bullet in the back of the head, as sadly occurs too often in countries not far away from us, there are real grounds for alarm.

1

Yet it would be a mistake to under-estimate the extent of the malaise currently affecting government here in the United Kingdom. While the public may have laughed at cartoons of Gladstone, Lloyd George, Churchill or Atlee, they knew the significance of the political choices presented by the leaders of those times and, insofar as they were enfranchised, they participated to a high degree in elections. In short, they overwhelmingly believed that voting made a difference. By contrast, no fewer than one in three of those eligible to vote did not take part in the 2015 general election, even though the outcome was expected to be very close. Add in the very significant number of citizens not even included on the election register, and the participation rate is even lower. As Table 1.1 illustrates, the decline in the proportion of electors exercising their democratic rights in UK general elections since 1950 is both striking and alarming. It is thought to reflect at least in part a growing perception that voting doesn't make a difference – the view articulated by Russell Brand in the lead-up to the 2015 poll, and repeated, as political activists will testify, on countless doorsteps in the course of the campaign. The degree of disaffection appears particularly marked among younger electors, who are least likely to cast a vote. But for the disproportionate impact of older voters, the overall figures in Table 1.1 would look even worse.

Why are so many people opting out of the political process? There are many suggested explanations – some more convincing that others – but three broad themes emerge, albeit with considerable overlaps between them. First there is strong evidence of public distrust of politicians. This was brought into sharp relief by the expenses scandal but was already a serious factor beforehand, and is unlikely simply to fade with the passage of time. Second is a growing sense of alienation between those engaged in the political process and the public, as though politicians were different from the rest of society rather than representing it. Third is a widening gap between public expectations and what realistically can be delivered, reinforcing disillusionment at the perceived failure of politicians to deliver for their electorate.

Table 1.1: Population and electoral statistics, 1950–2015

Year	Electorate	Votes cast	Turnout %	18+ population	Unregistered population
1950	34,412,255	28,771,124	83.6		
1951	34,919,331	28,596,594	81.9		
1955	34,852,179	26,759,729	76.8		
1959	35,397,304	27,862,652	78.7		
1964	35,894,054	27,657,148	77.1		
1966	35,957,245	27,264,747	75.8		
1970	39,342,013	28,344,798	72.0		
1974 (February)	39,753,863	31,340,162	78.8		
1974 (October)	40,072,970	29,189,104	72.8		
1979*	41,095,649	31,221,362	76.0	41,885,600	789,951
1983	42,192,999	30,671,137	72.7	42,382,100	189,101
1987	43,180,753	32,529,578	75.3	43,528,600	347,847
1992	43,275,316	33,614,074	77.7	44,413,800	1,138,484
1997	43,846,152	31,286,284	71.4	44,820,300	974,148
2001	44,403,238	26,367,383	59.4	45,756,100	1,352,862
2005	44,245,939	27,148,510	61.4	47,162,700	2,916,761
2010	45,597,461	29,687,604	65.1	49,371,100	3,773,639
2015	46,382,192	30,697,279	66.2	50,909,100	4,526,908

Note: * Population figures by age are unavailable for 1979, thus the figures in the last two columns correspond to the 1981 population estimates.

Sources: Rawlings, C. and Thrasher, M. and Cole, D. (2012) *British Electoral Facts 1832–2012*, London: Biteback Publishing; Office for National Statistics, mid-year population estimates.

These three interlocking themes require further examination. One frequently heard refrain in discussions about contemporary British politics is that ideological divisions that used to distinguish political parties have been eroded to the point where 'today's politicians are all the same'. A sting in the tail is often added – 'they are only in it for themselves'. While there were significant differences between the policies on offer from the main political parties contesting the 2015 British general election, it is certainly true that the sharp ideological divides that were seen to underpin most 20th-century political debates have been smoothed over in the search for the middle ground that is now widely recognised as critical to electoral success. Indeed it is ironic that today's political strategists often search for 'dividing lines' to distinguish them from their opponents – a mission that would have been considered unnecessary half a century earlier.

There is something of a paradox here, for another opinion often voiced by the public is frustration at the tendency of politicians to bad-mouth their opponents. 'Why can't they stop bickering and instead start working together in the common interest?' Indeed the formation of the Conservative–Liberal Democratic Coalition government in 2010 appeared to play well, at least in its early days, with the public's desire to see politicians burying the hatchet in the common interest. Yet the outcome of the 2015 general election, and in particular the disastrous showing of the Lib Dems, appears to point to an opposite conclusion. If having to compromise on key party priorities (such as opposition to student tuition fees) as part of a coalition agreement results in a catastrophic rout at the subsequent general election, what possible incentive can there be for politicians to seek the middle ground? Indeed it is difficult to see many willing takers for a junior coalition-partner role if a future general election fails to deliver an outright majority.

The Lib Dems were not alone in being punished for cooperating with another party. Labour's Scottish meltdown can also be attributed in a large degree to its participation in the 'Better Together' campaign opposing Scottish independence in the 2014 referendum. This left Labour vulnerable to the 'Red Tories' jibe so effectively deployed by the Scottish National Party (SNP). The election of Jeremy Corbyn as Labour leader in the aftermath of Labour's 2015 general election defeat has been widely interpreted as reflecting a search by Labour Party members for a more 'authentic' leader who has 'stuck to his principles' rather than sought to control the central ground. Only in Northern Ireland, where memories of the 'Troubles' are still fresh and strong enough to counter other pressures, is there still a clear public appetite for parties to work together across the traditional divides.

While on the surface there appears to be a contradiction between public attitudes to politicians either working together or sticking to their principles, in reality both are the product of growing public distrust. Today's politicians are increasingly seen as a homogenous group, having more in common with each other than with the world outside the 'Westminster Bubble'. Although Peter Oborne overstates his case in *The Triumph of the Political Class*[2] there is nevertheless an underlying truth in his analysis of the changing make-up of today's Westminster politicians. Whereas in the 1950s and 1960s Members of Parliament tended to be older, to have had significant 'real world' experience before being elected and to come from markedly different backgrounds (typically the armed forces and business on the Conservative benches, trade unions and academia on Labour's side), today's MPs are younger, have less experience of working outside the political world and tend to have reached Westminster by similar routes (university, working for an MP or a think-tank). If political ambition appears to be the common driving force of many modern careers at Westminster it is hardly surprising if a disenchanted public yearn nostalgically for a supposed golden age when politicians were more obviously different from each other and yet could (witness the very effective war-time coalition) come together when necessary in the national interest.

Of course there are wider trends at work, including the decline of the traditional 'tribal' loyalties that used to bind electors more closely to their party, to which they demonstrated unwavering loyalty through thick and thin. By contrast, the more transactional approach of today leads electors increasingly to judge parties on how their policies are likely to impact on the voters' interests. Indeed nostalgia for the certainties of the more tribal politics of the mid-20th century may also reflect a sense of loss as electors no longer see the party they traditionally supported as representing their interest. The emotional appeal of protest parties such as the UK Independence Party (UKIP) is very much founded on providing a refuge for electors who no longer feel at home in the party for which they used to vote. This appeal to the disaffected is all the greater if these protest parties can present Parliament and its members as 'different from us' – an alien, metropolitan class, out of touch with people at the grassroots. This was not just a UKIP message. The SNP's extraordinary capture of all except three parliamentary seats in Scotland was equally founded on the message that it alone would stand up for Scotland's interests against an indifferent or even hostile Westminster. Indeed, with the combination of low levels of participation in the ballot and a first-past-the-post voting system delivering majority governments that command the support of less than a quarter of the electorate, public disaffection seems likely to intensify.

There is a further paradox here in that, by comparison with the supposed golden age of the immediate post-war period, MPs today are much more visible in their constituencies and are far more extensively involved in local case-work. There is some evidence[3] suggesting that the public's attitudes towards their local MP are more favourable than to MPs as a whole. This may well reflect recognition of work undertaken in the constituency by the sitting MP. However, the personal vote still accounts for only a relatively small proportion of the total votes cast, as the huge swings in 2015 that carried away the vast majority of Lib Dem Members across the country and Labour Members in Scotland demonstrated. Even MPs who had exceptional reputations as local representatives were swept away by the national tide.

The negative perceptions of politicians, government and Parliament have almost certainly been reinforced in recent years by a series of highly publicised failures to implement new policy initiatives efficiently and cost-effectively. In their masterful study *The blunders of our governments*,[4] King and Crewe provide a damning catalogue of failure by Conservative, Labour and Coalition governments from the 1980s up to the very recent past. From the Poll Tax, through the mis-selling of private pensions, the disastrous introduction of the Child Support Agency, the short-lived but humiliating saga of Britain's membership of the European Exchange Rate Mechanism, the failed public-private partnership for upgrading the London Underground, the botched introduction of new European Farming Subsidies, numerous information technology (IT) contracts across a swathe of government departments and the costly and unnecessary reorganisation of the National Health Service (NHS), to the creation of unwanted Police and Crime Commissioners, the landscape of government is littered with expensive, high-profile failures. None of this does any good to the reputation of government and those who aspire to it.

One of the most powerful criticisms of modern government in the UK is the extent to which politicians escape the consequences of their failures. Very few of the blunders highlighted by King and Crewe led to the resignation or dismissal of the responsible minister. This partly reflected the very short tenure of most ministers, who are often lucky to stay two years in their job before being moved on. This ministerial merry-go-round has become an accepted feature of modern political life, with the accompanying expectation of annual reshuffles. This is damaging to good government in a number of ways. If ministers do not expect to be in post for more than a year or two, they will inevitably focus their attention on short-term initiatives that may win them plaudits, even if these are unlikely to bring lasting benefits to the country. At the same time, difficult and unpopular but necessary causes requiring long-term commitment can easily be put on the back burner and left for a future minister to take the flak. Furthermore, ministers who do not expect to be around to answer for how a policy has been implemented in, say, five or ten years time, may not choose to give the detailed attention necessary to ensure that the policy is properly thought through.

Apart from these perverse disincentives to good government, the ministerial merry-go-round illustrates only too clearly how the way that Westminster operates is far removed from the practice of most other organisations. In October 2013 the three main British political parties all changed their housing spokesperson on the same day! I knew all three well and spoke to each of them in the days following the reshuffle. They all told the same curious story: their party leader had reassured each of them that the move was not a comment on their performance or ability but simply reflected the need for a change in the appearance of the party's front-bench team.

What business would survive such a reshuffle, repeated annually, of its senior and middle management based not on performance but on appearance? A further unfortunate consequence of the rapid turnover of ministers and front-benchers is the obstacle this creates to good working relationships between politicians and the sectors for which they are, or may become, responsible. Knowing the key players in an industry or public service, and understanding the likely impact of political or economic decisions on their sector, is crucial to good policy development and implementation. By contrast, far too many senior figures in a huge range of private, public and voluntary organisations currently feel out of touch with the politicians responsible for their sector and the processes by which their policies are developed. This all reinforces the sense of a separate 'political class' who play by different rules to the rest of society.

Of course, politicians do have to handle more intrusive media challenges than those engaged in most other walks of life, but this is not a reason to suspend the normal criteria that most well-run organisations would see as essential to the efficient delivery of their goods and services. Nor is this much more intensive media scrutiny an excuse for failure. It is certainly true that in a world where 24/7 media coverage, Freedom of Information requests and social media comment inevitably expose ministers to relentless detailed scrutiny, government blunders are more likely to be exposed than in the past, when they might have remained undetected until relevant government papers were made public 30 years after the event. But it is fanciful to think that we can, let alone, should, return to the less-intrusive media environment of the past. Government today has to operate in the full, unforgiving glare of the media spotlight, and it therefore has to be better at avoiding the often elementary mistakes catalogued by King and Crewe.

While government today is more exposed to media scrutiny than in the past, it is also true that there has been an exponential growth in the attention given by ministers to the presentation of their policies. Government has become much more focused on, and adept at, putting the best possible gloss on its actions – witness the careers of Bernard Ingham and Alastair Campbell. But, if King and Crewe are correct, then all this has been to little avail, as their book suggests that since the 1980s governments have been more blunder prone than in the past. Could these processes be linked? Is it possible that in trying to shape policy responses to be better received in the media, politicians may be unwittingly making themselves more vulnerable to the very criticism they are seeking to avoid? In seeking to present a media-friendly solution to a problem, and often aiming to do so at speed in response to media pressure, could government actually be compounding the problem? The Dangerous Dogs Act 1991 is often quoted as bad policy arising from an over-hasty knee-jerk reaction to a media call for 'something to be done'. This is not a lone example. Nor is it just a case of speed prompting bad decision making. The attitude of mind that attaches a higher importance to how a policy will play in the media, rather than how it will work in practice, also leads down the same unhappy path.

An instructive example is the way in which the mansion tax proposal emerged. This was originally advocated by the Lib Dems but was taken up by the Labour Party and presented as a means of raising funds for the NHS in the run-up to the 2015 general election. The underlying problem that led to a proposed 'super tax' on properties worth more than £2 million is the current unfair and unsatisfactory impact of property taxation. Because of the way the Council Tax is assessed, millionaire owners of huge homes in highly affluent areas can, perversely, end up paying no more, and in some circumstances less, Council Tax than families in modest homes in poorer areas. This reflects both the design of the Council Tax and the failure to update it since its introduction in 1991, during which time the gap between the highest and lowest value properties in England has widened massively. The obvious policy response is to bring the Council Tax up to date to reflect today's property values, and with a wider range of bands. This would not just remedy the unfairness in existing arrangements; it would also provide an (admittedly modest) counter to house price inflation by increasing Council Tax liability in higher-value properties.

However, politicians of all persuasions have shied away from this sensible policy response. The reason is a fear of adverse publicity, with electoral consequences – for it would be very tempting and easy for opposition parties and the media to run scare stories about huge, threatened Council Tax increases once revaluation was mentioned. I write this with some feeling, having, as Local Government Minister, taken legislation through Parliament in 2003 to introduce regular ten-yearly revaluations of Council Tax and allow the creation of additional bands, only to see this legislation repealed by my successor after I left government in 2005. So the scheduled 2007 revaluation never occurred, Council Tax continues to be based on notional 1991 property values and only in Wales has an additional band been added.

The mansion tax was a classic politicians' response to the conundrum of how to raise additional revenue from a group of households who unquestionably could (and should) pay more than they do currently, without frightening the majority of Council Tax payers. They hoped to achieve this by creating a new tax that applied to only a small group of people occupying very high-value properties. An added attraction for Westminster politicians was the hope that central government could pocket the proceeds, rather than local government, for whom the Council Tax has traditionally been the largest source of locally raised revenue. In the belief that the pledge to tax the super-rich would play well with the rest of the population, those who advocated the mansion tax overlooked the serious practical problems it would inevitably have caused – imposing a new, separately assessed property tax without reforming the existing one and leaving local government inadequately funded. It may have had political attractions (although this is certainly unproven), but it was profoundly bad policy making.

Traditionally, it has been the role of the civil service to 'iron out' incoherent or impractical political proposals to ensure that what is finally enacted is workable. But there is growing evidence that the ministerial–civil service relationship is under greater stress than in the past and is working less well than it should.[5] There have always been tensions. This is inevitable in a relationship between a permanent civil service there to serve the government of the day and politicians whose tenure is temporary. As a result, politicians can feel uncomfortable depending for advice on people who have in the past and may in the future be working with and for their political opponents. But since 1979 those tensions appear to have intensified, from the loyalty questioning in the Thatcher era ('Is he one of us?') to the frustration felt by some, but by no means all, in the Blair, Brown and Cameron governments at perceived obstructionism among some civil servants. There have also been growing questions about the capability of the civil service to deliver complex programmes or projects. And under the subsequent Coalition and Conservative governments, sharp downsizing in several departments has unquestionably eroded the capacity and collective memory of the civil service. There has also been a significant expansion in the role of Special

Advisors (SPADs), who may well contribute valuable specialist and political expertise, and so help good decision making, but at their worst can operate as an alternative power base, threatening the maintenance of good relations between ministers and senior civil servants.

All of these processes may help to explain what is widely perceived to be a growing reluctance on the part of civil servants to play their traditional role of 'speaking truth to power'. If pointing out the impracticalities of a much-cherished political objective might earn the civil servant the reputation of being 'awkward' or 'obstructive', and consequently might damage his or her promotion prospects, there will inevitably be temptations to keep quiet (or to acquiesce). One of my most chilling moments as a minister was being told by a senior civil servant that a particular option had not been included in a submission because, while the department believed it viable, they thought that Number 10 wouldn't like it.[6] It was all the more troubling because the secretary of state, John Prescott, had made it clear on countless occasions to his departmental civil servants that while he would seek the Prime Minister's views as appropriate, he did not expect his officials' advice to be coloured by the views of Number 10 SPADs (whom he often described disparagingly as 'teenyboppers') claiming to be speaking for the PM. Once civil servants begin to adapt their advice to take account of what they believe the most senior politicians want to hear, they are on a slippery slope that undermines the Northcote-Trevelyan foundations, on which the ethos of British government has depended for a century and a half.

Of course, it is not only the civil service that should be challenging policy proposals to ensure that they are sound and practicable; that too is the role of Parliament. In theory, any new government policy should be subject to detailed scrutiny in the course of its passage through the House of Commons and House of Lords, so that potential weaknesses and flaws can be identified and corrected. To an extent this process acts as a check on ill-considered measures being implemented, but there are powerful countervailing forces working in the opposite direction. This is the almost inevitable consequence of Parliament's dual role of, on the one hand, providing the government of the day and, on the other, holding that government to account.

When a government commands a majority in the House of Commons there is a natural instinct for it to want to use that majority to ensure the easiest and quickest passage of its legislation through the House. So there is an inevitable tendency for the government whips to want their party's representatives on Public Bill and Statutory Instrument Committees to support the government at all times and reject all opposition amendments. As the whips control appointments to those committees and exercise a powerful influence on individual MPs' promotion prospects, it takes a very determined backbencher to break ranks and support an amendment that is likely to improve the legislation when that amendment has been proposed by the opposition. Timetabling arrangements in Committee can also result in curtailed opportunity for scrutiny and debate, as previously did the use of guillotine motions.

So too often, new measures pass through the House of Commons without adequate scrutiny, even if the processes are theoretically there to identify and remedy the defects. When the Bill reaches the House of Lords, where the government of the day does not necessarily enjoy a majority, unwelcome amendments to legislation can be countered by reference to the doctrine of the primacy of the elected chamber. The occasions on which sensible Lords amendments are overturned when the Bill returns to the Commons on the basis that the unelected house cannot be allowed to prevail are too numerous to list. Later in this book, I will propose some changes that could be made to the parliamentary procedures to improve the scrutiny of legislation and make it more likely that flaws are identified and corrected. However, we also have to return to the question of why it is that government is so prone to failure.

One of the key factors is the growing gap between public expectation and what, in reality, national governments can deliver. The process of globalisation and the growth of supra-national institutions have inevitably constrained the ability of individual nation-states to determine their future in isolation from the wider economic and political environment in which they operate. At the same time the extension of social media and the move towards a more presidential style of politics in the UK have tended to magnify public expectations of what one individual may achieve. These forces are, of course, pulling in opposite directions. So at a time when governments are in a number of respects much more fettered in their capacity to act, the public are subject to ever more simplistic exhortations. 'Sign up to this campaign', 'send this tweet or text message', 'add your name to our e-petition' is the message, with the implication that this will be sufficient to effect change.

This is, let's be clear, not a criticism of campaigning. Campaigns have always been the lifeblood of democratic politics and it is absolutely right that people who feel strongly about an issue should be encouraged and helped to get their message over to their elected representatives. Petitions have been an integral part of the campaigning process for centuries. So, in one sense we should be delighted that it is now so much easier to communicate, electronically, with our Members of Parliament, councillors or other elected representatives. In the interests of accountability MPs must be answerable to their constituents and must know what are the priorities and concerns of those who have put them into office. Equally, the public should expect and receive regular, meaningful feedback on what their elected representatives are doing, what are the constraints preventing them from achieving more and how they plan to tackle and, if possible, overcome those obstacles. This dialogue is crucial to an effective democracy and is potentially more achievable in modern society, where electronic media have greatly increased the options for two-way communications.

However, there is a downside. While new media have extended the opportunities for communication, they have also tended to over-simplify the options and implications of particular decisions. The limited number of characters that can be included in a tweet or text message is one constraint. So too is the pressure to give an instant rather than a considered response. Indeed those MPs who fail to give a rapid reply, perhaps because the issue requires further research and consideration before they commit themselves, are open to the charge of 'dithering', or being 'behind the curve'. Yet in a complex modern society where a huge number of interests, organisations or relevant factors often need to be taken into account before a properly informed decision can be reached, the pressure for rapid responses can very easily result in comments that are later seen as being embarrassing and may be used to imply inconsistency or betrayal. We have yet to find a way to benefit from the potential of new technology to improve two-way communication between the public and their representatives without at the same time dumbing down the conversation.

The problem is compounded by the highly centralised nature of government in England, in which a surprisingly large proportion of decisions have been retained at a national level rather than being devolved to regional or local bodies. This has had three main consequences. First, it has tended to reinforce the perception that all power is concentrated in Westminster, so fuelling unrealistic expectations of what government can deliver. Second, it has undermined the ability of local government to act as a powerful representative body for its local community. Third, it has contributed to the problem of 'overload' in Whitehall and Westminster, with ministers and civil servants struggling to see through a veritable blizzard of regulations and order-making powers, many of which have no strategic significance and could easily be devolved to a lower tier of government. At a time when government has been subject to harsh criticism for its failures and blunders, the case for doing less and doing it better is a strong one.

However, this will require facing down the political and media pressure for government to be seen to be in charge of every issue in every part of the country. It is all too easy for arguments to be advanced for government intervention to tackle local problems. If a particularly tragic case of a failure of child protection or neglect of the elderly is exposed, it is almost invariably accompanied by a call for the government to intervene, even though responsibility for children's services and adult social care rests with the local authority. The problem is compounded by the relatively small size of England and the disproportionate influence of national as against local or regional media, which are far more influential in America and many parts of continental Europe. Even if we pay lip-service to the principle of localism, our politicians and media seem pathologically incapable of resisting calls to put an end to so-called 'post code lotteries', where the standard of service is seen to vary unacceptably from one area to another. So, for example, we saw Eric Pickles, former Secretary of State for Communities and Local Government, proclaiming his adherence to localism while at the same time lecturing local councils on the frequency of their refuse collection services.

This is not to say that there will not be occasions when intervention by central government is necessary, either because the scale of the problem is too great to be tackled successfully by a local authority on its own, or where the persistent failure by that local authority to meet its responsibilities will be remedied only through outside intervention. The case studies in the chapters that follow include several illustrations of interventions by central government that, in my view, were both necessary and appropriate. The distinction between a necessary intervention that leaves lasting benefits and inappropriate or capricious interference that undermines local capacity and confidence and leaves a negative legacy is not always clear or easily defined. One of the most difficult challenges for those involved in the process of government is to understand the level at which responsibility is best discharged and to seek outcomes that support an appropriate division of powers between different tiers of government.

The devolution of power to Scotland, Wales and Northern Ireland has effectively created a fire-wall preventing inappropriate interventions by Westminster politicians in devolved matters. However, no similar framework has been established in England, with the partial exception of London, where the creation of the mayoralty and Greater London Authority (GLA) has established a region-wide authority able and sometimes willing to challenge central government's attempts to call all the shots. However, it has not been able, nor has it sought, to prevent central intervention in the affairs of individual London boroughs. This reflects the deliberate separation of powers between the GLA and the boroughs in London, which did not give the GLA a supervisory role. Devolving power to the lowest level at which it can sensibly be exercised is a sensible general objective, but it must be tempered by a practical understanding of the consequences, and the establishment of safeguards to ensure that the greater public interest is not sacrificed by local decision making that turns a blind eye to wider obligations. This theme emerges repeatedly in the pages that follow.

Finding the right balance between local, regional and national tiers of government is not just an issue for national government. Backbench MPs find it extraordinarily hard to resist wading into local debates, often seeing this as an opportunity to burnish their own public relations image by attacking an unpopular action taken by the local authority without acknowledging that the formal responsibility for the relevant service lies with the local council. While this may win them 'brownie points' with their local electorate in the short term, it is damaging to the operation of a mature, devolved democracy by perpetuating the myth that Parliament is the body ultimately controlling everything. Until government and MPs recognise that they should focus only on national and strategic priorities, allow decision making on most other matters to be fully devolved and resist public pressure to intervene indiscriminately in devolved matters, we will, I fear, continue to inhabit a world where unreal expectations are raised about the power of government – expectations that will inevitably lead to disappointment and disillusion.

Having said all this, it would be wrong for me to paint an unduly pessimistic picture of the processes of government in the UK. Despite the many problems and pressures working in a negative direction, there is still much that is effective and admirable about the British system of government. As almost all commentators acknowledge, Britain is a society where policy making remains largely free of corruption and where the public are able to comment on and influence the evolution of policy in most areas of activity. There have been significant advances in recent years in facilitating public access to information that previously would have been withheld – through, in particular, the Freedom of Information Act. It is important to keep a sense of perspective. As well as highly publicised failures there have been many success stories in recent years, some predictable, others delivering surprisingly positive outcomes, given the constraints that had to be overcome. It is also the case that most of those who get involved in the political process and stand for public office in the UK do so primarily for altruistic reasons. They want to change society for the better. This is not to say that other motives, some less worthy, do not also come into play, nor to deny that politicians can at times act capriciously or adopt a narrowly partisan approach. But, despite that, there is still a strong British tradition, encapsulated in the Nolan principles,[7] of working in the public interest and using power not for personal gain but to advance the prospects and improve the living conditions of those whom politicians are elected to serve. So, while we must understand and deal with the forces that are working against good policy making, we also need to acknowledge and learn from positive influences and achievements. In the chapters that follow I seek to do both.

For almost half a century I have observed and participated in many of the processes of government in the UK, locally, regionally and nationally. I have been involved in campaigning for change from outside government and responding as a minister to others' campaigns. I have worked in the voluntary sector, served as a local councillor, represented two different London constituencies in Parliament for around a quarter of a century and served as a minister in government for eight years. From that experience I have distilled a series of case studies on the process of translating policy into practice that comprise the next nine chapters of this book. Each examines different aspects of the policy-making and implementation process. The aim is, through exploring the detailed implications of each of these case studies, to highlight broader conclusions that can help to point to ways in which we can do better in the future, both by addressing the problems and learning from the successes. One of the lessons I have learned is the extent to which apparently new problems can often reflect, sometimes in a different guise, challenges that have occurred previously and have taxed the brains of an earlier generation of politicians and administrators. This is not to say that there is nothing new under the sun, nor to echo the pessimism of the Roman Emperor Marcus Aurelius, who believed that a man aged 40 had probably experienced all that there was to see in the world, as supposedly new developments simply repeated previous patterns.[8] However, our era is more prone to the opposite mistake of assuming that today's challenges are unique and there is little or nothing to be learned from the past. Through more than 40 years' worth of experiences as set out in the following chapters, there are many common and persisting themes that are just as relevant now as they were years ago. Indeed the seeds of so many of the major issues that tax today's policy makers can be found all too clearly in the patterns of past decision making or decision avoiding. The case studies in the following chapters are not, then, just of academic interest. At the very least they explain the context of many of today's challenges, and suggest ways in which we can avoid repeating past mistakes and capitalise on achievements. The final chapter pulls together those conclusions and makes recommendations on how we can govern better in 21st-century Britain.

TWO

Homelessness

In summer 1973 I went to work at the Shelter Housing Aid Centre (SHAC), a London-wide housing project led by the inspirational Father Paul Byrne. SHAC had emerged from the pioneering work of the Catholic Housing Aid Society, which aimed to help families facing housing problems to secure the most appropriate solution. At the time the housing market was dominated by three tenures – two expanding and one in apparently terminal decline. Access to the two growing tenures, owner-occupation and council housing, was tightly controlled by lending or letting criteria, operated, respectively, by building societies and banks on the one hand, and by local authorities on the other, with the two sectors operating in almost total isolation from each other. Access to the declining private rented sector was more open, but conditions were often poor, exploitation was rife and the tenure was seen as an option of last resort.

In this context, SHAC's aim was to assist individuals and families to find whatever solution was best for them, rather than checking whether they met the criteria for access to just one specific tenure. It was a people-focused service, exploring whatever options might be available and appropriate to the family concerned and acting when necessary as their advocate. So, its work included:

- innovative schemes to help middle- to low-income households access homeownership;
- help in securing New Town housing for those willing and able to move;

- referrals to the emerging new wave of housing associations beginning to make an impact in some of London's most disadvantaged areas;
- intervention to secure improvements in insanitary premises;
- help and advocacy for tenants threatened with eviction or harassment;
- advocacy with local authorities on behalf of applicants whose needs might not have been fully assessed; and
- action to help homeless people get a roof over their heads.

   The fact that SHAC was able to provide such a comprehensive service was due to the successful fundraising of Shelter, which had been launched in 1966 and had rapidly achieved a high profile by exposing the extent of housing deprivation and homelessness in a supposedly affluent society. Des Wilson, Shelter's first director, brilliantly seized the opportunity, in the aftermath of the screening of Jeremy Sandford's remarkable television programme 'Cathy Come Home', to publicise the sufferings and misfortunes of families like Cathy's, and in doing so raised very substantial sums from public donations to support the work of housing associations and of innovative housing projects.

   In the course of my first few weeks at SHAC, working as an advocate for homeless families, it became all too clear that Cathy's grim story was in no way unusual or exceptional. Policy for the relief of homelessness in Britain had effectively been left in a time warp, and still reflected the judgemental and punitive attitudes of the Victorian Poor Law. So, housing the homeless was not seen as an integral part of the work of council housing departments. Instead, the obligations, such as there were, to assist homeless people applied to social services departments and required them only to:

> provide temporary accommodation for persons in urgent need thereof, being need arising in circumstances that could not reasonably have been foreseen, or in any other circumstances as the authority may in any particular case determine.[1]

The inadequacy of this provision was self-evident. It implied that only temporary help was needed, even though authoritative reports commissioned by the Labour government in the late 1960s had demonstrated that a shortage of suitable permanent accommodation, particularly in high-stress areas such as London, was a major factor contributing to a rising tide of homelessness.[2] Indeed, the phrase 'circumstances that could not reasonably have been foreseen' reflected the late 1940s' view that this provision would primarily be needed to help people made homeless in an emergency such as fire or flooding. For them, only temporary accommodation would be needed, as they would normally expect to return to their home once the damage had been made good. The second phrase 'any other circumstances as the authority may in any particular case determine', gave total discretion to the local welfare authority, which in many parts of the country was separate from the authority responsible for housing, to decide who might benefit from its assistance. This discretion allowed the continuation of harsh policies dating back to the Poor Law era, when the homeless were generally seen as either feckless, and therefore fit only for the workhouse, or vagrants, who were normally driven out of the parish. It is indeed one of the curious ironies of legislation that the 1948 National Assistance Act, which opened with the ringing statement 'The Poor Law shall cease to have effect', actually consigned a generation of homeless families to the indignities of the former Poor Law institutions, many of which were adapted for use as temporary accommodation. In line with Poor Law practice, husbands and male partners were regularly excluded, as accommodation in many areas was confined to women and children only. Similarly, assistance was routinely refused to homeless families thought to have come from another area, on the grounds that they were not local residents and therefore did not merit local accommodation.

The inadequacy of the statutory provision at this time was well summarised by Donnison and Ungerson in their authoritative study of housing policy:

> The 1948 Act provided the wrong powers (imposing a weak obligation to provide temporary shelter for

small numbers, when the problem of homelessness called for strong obligations to provide permanent housing for large numbers) and those powers were in the wrong hands (resting ineffectually with the DHSS [Department of Health and Social Security] and the County Social Services departments instead of the DoE [Department of the Environment] and the District housing authorities).[3]

Why did this manifestly unsatisfactory situation persist for so long, and why did government not act sooner to remedy it? There are a number of answers. The first is the lack of any strong political pressure for change. The homeless were a small minority without significant political clout. Like many other small minorities, they struggled to gain public attention or support. Second, their exclusion from mainstream housing provision reflected a widely held view that homelessness was a social problem caused by personal inadequacy rather than problems of access to housing. The homeless were often associated with alcohol abuse and other social problems, which made it easy to treat them as separate from the rest of society. It was therefore hardly surprising that many local councillors and housing managers saw homeless applicants as distinct from others in housing need and were concerned that they should not 'jump the queue' for housing. As Donnison and Ungerson record:

> When John Greve's researchers sought their first interview with the London County Council's Housing department, the opening words of the man deputed to deal with them were 'Very well, but tell me what has homelessness to do with housing?'[4]

The extent to which the homeless were seen as a threat rather than as a group of people in need of housing was well conveyed by the view of one local authority housing officer quoted by Bryan Glastonbury in another report commissioned by government at that time:

'I have to pay attention to the ordinary standards of decent people. We don't want these dead-legs. They muck up the books and make life a misery for ordinary folks.'[5]

Despite clear evidence that the number of homeless families was rising significantly in the late 1950s and 1960s and that this reflected housing shortages and evictions from insecure private lettings rather than just problems of personal inadequacy, the old Poor Law prejudices were still alive and well in late 1960s' Britain. With no political or institutional pressure for change, the old, inappropriate statutory provision might well have been allowed to stagger on for many more years, but for an unexpected event that galvanised the one group capable of building a momentum for change. The trigger was a late amendment to a routine Local Government Act in 1972, introduced as a 'tidying-up' measure. This changed the (weak) duty in the 1948 National Assistance Act to a discretionary power. Inadequate as the old duty had been, it was nevertheless seen by voluntary agencies working with homeless people as one of the very few weapons they could deploy on behalf of their homeless clients. I well remember referring to it in discussion with local authority officers reluctant to accept an application from a homeless family.

When the voluntary agencies became aware of the change in the law, our response was to launch a campaign that was ultimately to lead to the 1977 Housing (Homeless Persons) Act. Five voluntary organisations came together under the name of the Joint Charities Group with the aim of promoting an amendment to the next Local Government Bill to reinstate the 1948 Act's duty (the five were CHAR, the Campaign for the Homeless and Rootless, represented by Nick Beacock; CHAS, the Catholic Housing Aid Society, represented by Bob Kahn and later Robina Rafferty; CPAG, the Child Poverty Action Group, represented by Henry Hodge; SHAC, the London Housing Aid Centre, represented by myself; and Shelter, represented by Bob Widdowson). Other voluntary organisations joined as the campaign progressed. Although unsuccessful in this first objective, the campaign attracted significant media interest and support from MPs, which in turn prompted responses from both government and opposition. The then Conservative government, rattled by criticism that it was weakening protection for homeless people, issued two circulars in response. The first, to social service authorities, effectively reinstated the duty of the 1948 Act. The second, a joint circular issued by DoE and the DHSS, set out a series of recommendations for best practice in responding to the needs of the homeless and also made clear the government's view that primary responsibility for the relief of homelessness should progressively transfer from social services to housing authorities. Shortly after this circular (Circular 18/74) was issued, the February general election resulted in a change of government and the incoming Secretary of State for the Environment, Antony Crosland, announced a review that would consider the need for new legislation covering the functions of both housing and social service authorities for the relief of homelessness.

The story of the following three years leading up to the passage of the 1977 Housing (Homeless Persons) Act is a long one that has been told elsewhere,[6] and so there is no need to repeat it here, but there are a series of lessons that can be drawn from the process.

The first is the need for a catalyst to prompt reform in policy areas where there is no political or institutional pressure for change. In this case it was the voluntary organisations in contact with homeless people, and well informed about the way in which existing policies were working (or rather not working), who provided the catalyst. Their success depended, crucially, on their ability to exercise influence in three key ways.

1. *Political.* In the absence of strong political pressure for reform (because of the degree to which the homeless were seen as marginal and a problem), the Joint Charities Group was able to build a base of support among individual MPs and peers who were sympathetic to the cause and willing to speak on the subject when it was raised in Parliament. This of course raises the very interesting question of how far a charity may reasonably go in promoting the interests of the people it is working for without crossing the fine line between 'informed comment' and 'undue political pressure'.

This has been the subject of frequent debate over the years, with the attitude of the political parties tending to vary, often reflecting whether they are in government or opposition. The Coalition government elected in 2010 initially gave considerable emphasis to the concept of the 'Big Society', envisaging a larger role for voluntary and charitable organisations in the delivery of a range of public services. This inevitably implies an on-going dialogue between such organisations and those holding political and governmental office. The suggestion that voluntary organisations should limit themselves to 'good works' and make no comment on the impact of government policy and legislation that they are involved in implementing is, frankly, absurd. Yet within a relatively short period of time the Coalition government's enthusiasm for the 'Big Society' had noticeably waned and by the end of the Parliament it was legislating to restrict the scope for voluntary organisations to comment on political issues. This maladroit attempt to 'gag' independent comment on the impact of government policy reflected badly on the motives of the government and will make it difficult to resurrect a credible version of the notion of a 'Big Society'.

2. *Media.* One of the ways in which the Joint Charities Group succeeded in keeping the issue alive when others would happily have seen it brushed under the carpet was its ability to get high-profile media coverage. Shelter had shown the way in the late 1960s and, with a wealth of shocking evidence to hand of the failings of the legislative framework, it was not hard to secure regular publicity for the cause. One example was the wide variation in local policies towards housing homeless women expecting a child. Circular 18/74 had advised local authorities that women who were vulnerable through pregnancy should be treated as a priority for assistance if homeless. However, the way that this was interpreted varied enormously. Most authorities applied an arbitrary date – for example, accepting responsibility once the pregnancy had reached the seventh month – but some refused help until a baby was born. Such cases, once brought to the attention of the media, were powerful illustrations of the inadequacy of the existing provision and reinforced the case for new legislation.

It is sobering to recall the extent of public sympathy at that time for those needing welfare support. Indeed, in the late 1970s it was still possible to secure widespread sympathetic media coverage for the homeless. I am less sure about how we would have fared in the much harsher and judgemental climate of today.

3. *The civil service.* The publication of Circular 18/74 had prompted closer contact between the voluntary agencies and the civil service, both in relation to its interpretation and because the voluntary sector had ample evidence that the good practice recommended was not being implemented in many parts of the country. So, during the review that the Secretary of State had announced in June 1974 a great deal of effort went into documenting, for the benefit of DoE, the wide variations in practice on the ground and the continuation of outdated and inappropriate responses. Not only did this present a forceful case for new legislation, but it also gave the civil servants access to much more information about what was happening than they could glean from local authority statistical returns and the evidence they received filtered through the local authority associations. The transfer of lead responsibility from DHSS to DoE had occurred only recently, and the DoE had traditionally adopted a 'hands off' approach towards local housing management practice. Indeed the local authority associations remained largely hostile to the pressure for new legislation that would inevitably reduce their members' discretion. But their case was constantly undermined by the well-documented evidence of inhumane and punitive practices persisting in many areas. When Antony Crosland announced the conclusion of the review in the autumn of 1975 he emphasised that 'three quarters of all authorities in England appear to take a rather limited view of their responsibilities'. His Housing Minister, Reg Freeson, stressed in the House of Commons that 'the Department will be enquiring further of those authorities whose returns disclosed that they sometimes (and in a few cases it appears invariably) have to split up families in temporary accommodation'. Given the increased likelihood of embarrassment to the government caused by media coverage of such practices, the department's

traditional non-interventionist stance on matters of local authority housing management was clearly untenable, and the case for new legislation unanswerable. It was a significant and interesting example of evidence-based policy making leading to a major shift in the balance between central direction and local discretion. The importance of the civil service's input both in the decision to legislate and in securing the passage of the Housing (Homeless Persons) Act cannot be over-emphasised. The civil service team, led by Jim Hannigan, deserved great credit for the way it saw through a difficult but important reform in very challenging circumstances.

One of the most problematic issues was provision for single homeless people. The pejorative view of the homeless as separate and problematic derived in large measure from stereotypes of single homeless people as vagrants prone to alcoholism or other social problems and often staying in 'spikes' or common lodging houses, immortalised in George Orwell's *Down and out in London and Paris*. Of course some homeless people did fall into that category, but there were many others simply looking for accommodation in a market where their traditional source of housing, the private rented sector, was in steep decline. The development of council housing had been predominantly focused on the needs of families, with the three-bedroom house or flat the archetypal provision. With primary responsibility for the relief of homelessness now transferring to local authorities it would be untenable to restrict assistance to families alone, while consigning the single and childless to a different regime. However, local authorities generally lacked the housing and the expertise to provide adequately for significant numbers of single homeless people. The response recommended in Circular 18/74 sought to reconcile the inherent tensions and conflicts.

> It should be possible to extend some form of help to all who are homeless, whether families with children, adult families or people living alone. In areas where the housing situation is particularly difficult however, it will not be possible to help all to the same extent and first claim on the resources available must be

given to the most vulnerable referred to in the
Circular [18/74] as 'priority groups'.

This inevitably begged questions that would be repeatedly be
raised over the coming years about the way in which the needs
of most single homeless people would be met. Indeed the issue
remains a live one today.

The fact that the legislation proceeded only by means of a
Private Member's Bill was also significant. Following Crosland's
announcement in autumn 1975, a government bill was drafted
and was expected to be introduced in the 1976–77 session of
Parliament. However, in the spring of 1976 Crosland moved to
the Foreign Office and Peter Shore took over as Secretary of State
for the Environment. Not only was he less obviously committed
than his predecessor to the need for legislation, but he represented
an area (Tower Hamlets) where the local authority was strongly
hostile to the imposition of any new obligations to assist the
homeless. So, when the anticipated Homelessness Bill failed to
appear in the government's 1976–77 legislative programme, the
Joint Charities Group moved quickly to identify a backbench
MP sympathetic to the cause who had drawn a high place in the
ballot for Private Members' Bills. Stephen Ross, Liberal MP for
the Isle of Wight, had already indicated his interest and pledged
to introduce a Bill. The Joint Charities Group began drafting
such a Bill but was pleasantly surprised when the civil service
persuaded its ministers that they should let Ross take over the
already drafted government Bill. The relationship between the
voluntary organisations and the civil service that had developed
over the previous three years now became even more crucial,
with Stephen Ross, the Bill's sponsor, depending on both to
provide advice and guidance as he steered the Bill through
potentially difficult parliamentary stages.

The Bill reached the statute book in July 1977 and came
into force by the end of the year. Although it had been subject
to some amendments in the course of its passage through
Parliament it remained in essence a statutory affirmation of the
approach recommended in Circular 18/74. It ensured the full
transfer of authority for the relief of homelessness from social
services to housing authorities and made it clear that the relief

of homelessness would be an integral part of council housing responsibilities. Thirty years on from the National Assistance Act, the Poor Law had finally ceased to have effect.

So, what has been its impact? As might have been expected, the number of homeless households and, in particular, homeless families assisted by local authorities rose significantly in the years following the implementation of the Act. Whereas 33,700 had been accepted in 1976 (the last full year before the new legislation came into effect), the number rose to 53,100 in 1978 and the rising trend continued through the 1980s. While temporary accommodation remained in use, and indeed was increasingly deployed in areas of housing stress, the majority of homeless families accepted by local authorities eventually found their way into secure council lettings. At the same time many of the punitive policies towards homeless families that had lingered on into the 1970s, such as the exclusion of male partners, disappeared. Although most single homeless people remained outside the local authority obligations to secure accommodation, there was significant progress through the 1980s and 1990s in ending the use of common lodging houses. Instead, more suitable smaller units, including many providing care and support, were developed, particularly by housing associations, whose role was expanding significantly at this time. The problem of rough sleeping also attracted much more focused attention through the 1990s and early 2000s, with real progress being made in reducing the numbers sleeping on the streets and in extending preventative services to head off the risk of homelessness. So, within 25 years of the introduction of the 1977 Act the numbers both of rough sleepers and of homeless applicants to local authorities were on a declining trend. This, unfortunately, was not sustained beyond the change of government in 2010.

There was also a significant change in local authority attitudes. Most of those who had campaigned vociferously against the 1977 Act when it was first proposed accepted the new framework with little protest. Many acknowledged that their fears had proved largely groundless, and also welcomed procedures to clarify responsibilities where households crossed local authority boundaries. Stigmatisation of homeless people did not disappear entirely; it would have been surprising if such deep-rooted prejudices had gone away overnight, but the closer integration of provision for the homeless within mainstream housing services proved an important advance in helping recognition that the majority of homeless families were not intrinsically different from others in housing need.

Eighteen months after the Act reached the statute book, the government changed. As the opposition to it had come predominantly from Conservative MPs and councils it might have been expected that the new government, led by Margaret Thatcher, would have sought to repeal the Act. There were some calls for this, but, following a protracted period of review, the government decided not to make any substantial changes. In part this reflected the extent to which the legislation had been accepted by the vast majority of local authorities. It must also have been seen as a potential hot potato – repeal could easily have resurrected images of the bad old days that had attracted such significant media attention. There was also probably a third factor, the significance of which was not fully understood until several years later. This was the degree to which the provisions of the Housing (Homeless Persons) Act accorded with the instinctive view of many Conservatives that social housing should be a safety net for the poor rather than a more universal tenure.

At the time when the Act came into force council housing accounted for over 30% of the country's total housing stock. Since the 1940s the former statutory limitations on provision to house only the 'working classes' had been repealed, and there was an assumption that council housing was potentially available to all, even if priority and allocation was generally given to those without alternative options. Owner-occupation had also been expanding, and in the immediate post-war era had overtaken private renting as the largest tenure. However, through the 1960s and 1970s large numbers of working households with good incomes were still choosing to rent from the council if they had the option. If not necessarily universal, council housing was still catering for a sizeable cross-section of the population. With the exception of individual stigmatised estates council housing was a long way away from being a residual tenure only for those with no other option.

That pattern was about to change radically in the 1980s. Whereas a political consensus had existed over the first three and a half post-war decades in favour of an expanded council housing stock, the Thatcher government took a very different approach. Investment in new council housing was progressively scaled back, such that the number of completions fell from 103,403 in 1975 to just 780 in 1995.[7] At the same time the existing stock of council homes was dramatically reduced through Right to Buy sales. The condition and attractiveness of council housing also deteriorated as a result of two parallel trends. As, generally, the more desirable properties, and in particular detached and semi-detached council houses, sold first, the proportion of the diminished stock accounted for by flats and maisonettes in multi-storey blocks increased significantly. At the same time investment in maintenance was also being squeezed. Many homes built in the 1950s and 1960s needed modernisation and improvement and a number of the high-rise blocks that had become an increasingly important part of the council stock from the 1970s onwards were proving unsatisfactory and required intervention. The problem was aggravated by poor standards of housing management in some areas, which allowed some estates to deteriorate without the need for remedial action being flagged up. Had the concept of asset management planning been understood and the proceeds of Right to Buy sales (even taking account of the generous discounts available to purchasers) been channelled back into maintenance and renovation as well as the construction of new homes, this problem could have been greatly reduced. However, government restrictions on the use of capital receipts, coupled with cutbacks in support for new investment and squeezed maintenance budgets, prevented this. The outcome was a growing problem of disrepair and neglect that in turn led to increasing stigmatisation of substantial parts of the remaining council housing stock, a problem that was not addressed until the Decent Homes Programme was introduced by the Labour government.

An increased proportion of lettings going to the poorest and most vulnerable, coupled with a declining stock and deteriorating conditions, was a recipe for disaster. Within a relatively short period of time the social housing sector changed from being perceived as a source of good-quality housing offering a step up in life, to a residualised tenure increasingly seen as a last resort for those with no other option. The failure of government in the 1980s and early 1990s to recognise the toxic consequences of these trends and to take remedial action before the problem reached a tipping point from which recovery would not be possible is one of the other key lessons of this period. It was not that the evidence was hidden; on the contrary, the scale of the problem became increasingly clear through the last two decades of the 20th century.

This highlights the weakness of arrangements for on-going appraisal of the impact of new legislation. The parliamentary process is heavily slanted towards the means by which legislation gets onto the statute book (although it does not always do this well, an issue to which I will return) but provides only limited opportunities for post-legislative scrutiny. Individual government departments may give some resource to assessing the impact of specific Bills and policy initiatives. Additionally Select Committees may choose to conduct enquiries into how specific pieces of legislation may have worked in practice. But there is no systematic framework for evaluating, as a matter of course, how each Act of Parliament met, or failed to meet, the objectives it was expected to deliver. On the contrary, parliamentary processes work strongly against such evaluations. There is an element of the treadmill in the process, under which each year's legislative programme has to be swept up to make way for the next. The continuous pressure to make time for new legislative measures works strongly against an adequate allocation of time to evaluate whether previous years' legislation actually did what it said on the tin.

Without more time being specifically reserved for such evaluations, it is difficult to see how this will happen because political pressures work strongly in the opposite direction. Governments are generally keen to promote their new policies and reluctant to undertake post mortems on measures that may not have been as successful as they had hoped. When governments change, the new ministers coming into office are generally keen to draw a line under the past and focus instead on their new plans and policies. Civil servants are often reluctant to emphasise useful or successful initiatives taken by a previous government, lest they appear less than enthusiastic about the new one. In this context it is very easy for a 'year zero' approach to be adopted based on the misguided but politically powerful argument that the previous government's record was poor (which is why it is no longer in office), and so nothing useful can be learned from its experience.

Yet, throughout the story told in this chapter effective measures to evaluate how policy was working in practice would almost certainly have made a significant difference. In the late 1960s and early 1970s evaluation would have revealed the inadequacy of the 1948 National Assistance Act framework. Indeed it could well have accelerated the reform process by several years. In the 1980s and 1990s it would have highlighted the growing problem of stigmatisation of council housing and the need to take remedial action to improve conditions on deteriorating estates. It would also have brought into sharper focus the growing problem of single homelessness and rough sleeping. In both instances effective parliamentary scrutiny of the impact of legislation and its changing context would have placed far greater pressure on government to acknowledge emerging problems at an earlier stage and promote appropriate responses.

What other conclusions can be drawn on the impact of the 1977 Act and the subsequent evolution of policy towards the homeless? By putting the relief of homelessness at the heart of housing authority responsibilities, the Housing (Homeless Persons) Act crystallised the key interfaces between policy, access and stock condition. Put simply, those households most at risk of homelessness (whether as a consequence of living in insecure accommodation or as a result of their family's needs or characteristics) are less likely to go through the homelessness channel if alternative options are relatively easily available or good preventative services are in place. So, if they know they will be able to access social housing through another channel within a relatively short period of time, they may well feel able to endure their unsatisfactory current accommodation for a little longer, or to persuade their family or friends to allow them to stay for a further period. Good preventative services, including debt advice or conciliation of a conflict with an existing landlord, can have a similar impact.

Conversely, where there is no such alternative prospect of getting rehoused or appropriate preventative interventions, homelessness may well be the outcome at an earlier stage. A further complication is the likely outcome of a household's application being accepted by the local authority. The prospect of a long period in temporary accommodation, generally recognised as the least appropriate solution both in social and in financial terms, may well have a deterrent effect on potential homeless applicants, as can the use of particularly unpopular or stigmatised accommodation for homeless applicants. However, where homeless applicants have no prospect of remaining in their existing home, if they have one, the impact of such 'punitive' policies is of course to reinforce the stigma.

The interpretation by the local authority of its obligations, for example, towards those not in priority need categories will also impact on the numbers to be housed, as can be clearly seen from the experience in Scotland, where more generous policies, leading to the abolition of the 'priority need' concept have contributed to a significant increase in the numbers of homeless households accepted by local authorities.[8]

The impact of these variables on either increasing or reducing the 'flow' of homeless applicants and on the use of particular options for their accommodation can be very significant, as has been seen in the trends in England in the early 21st century. From 2003 onwards as the preventative policies set out in the 2002 Homelessness Act came into effect, the numbers of homeless acceptances fell from 147,820 in 2003 to 49,290 in 2010, and the numbers in temporary accommodation fell over the same period from 94,620 to 48,010. This achievement is all the more notable, given that the same Act extended priority need categories to include further groups of young, single homeless people, albeit not to the same degree as occurred subsequently in Scotland. Sadly, those positive trends did not survive the change of government in 2010, since when there has been a significant rise both in the numbers of homeless acceptances and in the numbers in temporary accommodation. This indicates that good preventative policies alone cannot work without complementary policies for the provision of new social lettings. Impending homelessness cannot be indefinitely postponed in the absence of the prospect of a better housing solution in the foreseeable future.

It is also worth noting that the trends in rough sleeping have followed a similar pattern. Intensive intervention and preventative work under the Rough Sleepers Initiative from the 1990s onwards led to a significant reduction in the numbers recorded as sleeping rough in the early 21st century. However, since the impact of the recession in 2008, and the reduction in the supply of new social rented housing under the Coalition and Conservative governments since 2010, as well as cuts in benefit entitlements, the numbers have again been rising. While wider influences are at work here (a substantial number of rough sleepers are non-UK nationals who will have been particularly affected by immigration-related restrictions on access to housing and benefits), the general truth that preventative policies are effective, but insufficient on their own to resolve the problem, applies equally.

The overall conclusion that emerges is that the Housing (Homeless Persons) Act has made a very significant and generally very positive impact on the evolution of policy for the prevention and relief of homelessness in Britain, and in so doing has provided a framework that allows variation between the constituent parts of the UK. It has survived major shifts in housing policy over the decades that it has been in force, and has ensured that homelessness can never again be treated as a marginal issue of little relevance to housing policy. But, while the Act has clearly demonstrated that it is necessary (and the fact that it has survived without fundamental amendment or repeal provides solid proof of this), it is at the same time not sufficient to achieve the elimination of homelessness. That, of course, depends on an adequate supply of housing to meet the country's overall needs, available on terms that are within the reach of all members of society. These are the key issues for the next two chapters.

THREE

The irresistible rise of Housing Benefit

How to make decent-quality housing affordable to people on low or fluctuating incomes has been one of the challenges facing policy makers for a century or more and is no nearer a satisfactory solution today than it was in the 19th century. As we have seen with homelessness, the problem was for a period side-stepped by those responsible for providing philanthropic or municipal housing by the convenient assumption that their mission was to provide for the industrious working classes – who in today's political language would be called 'hard working families'. The very poor and those who could not be expected to sustain regular rent payments were literally beyond the pale.

This framework was clearly not sustainable, particularly as the public sector housing programme expanded dramatically in the inter-war and post-Second World War era, with large-scale slum-clearance activity removing the bulk of the cheap and squalid housing in which the poorest had previously been living. William Beveridge wrestled with the challenge of finding an appropriate means to cover housing costs as part of his profoundly influential proposals for social security in post-war Britain. The problem was the variation in housing costs by locality and tenure, as well as by size of accommodation, which made it impossible to devise a flat-rate level of benefit based on subsistence needs, as for other basic requirements such as food and clothing. Beveridge concluded that only a notional element for rent should be incorporated into his national insurance scheme, which inevitably led to a requirement for a 'top-up' from

National Assistance to enable those without a regular work-based income to meet their housing costs.

Whereas Beveridge had assumed that the need for such supplements would be limited in numbers, and would be required only to cover temporary income shortfall caused, for example, by unemployment, the reality proved very different and by the early 1980s (by which time National Assistance had been replaced by Supplementary Benefit) approaching three million households were in receipt of a housing supplement under this scheme.

In parallel, some local councils had begun to introduce local rent-rebate schemes, although the numbers receiving such benefits remained relatively small until the 1970s. This reflected two main trends. The first was the continuing focus on providing for working families. The second was a national subsidy regime that enabled, indeed incentivised, councils to provide new homes that could be let at relatively modest rents, well within the means of most households in paid employment. In 1971 the Conservative government led by Edward Heath proposed a fundamental change, arguing that it was more efficient to subsidise individuals rather than bricks and mortar. The Housing Finance Act envisaged a substantial increase in rent levels, accompanied by the introduction of a national Rent Rebate scheme that would enable those on relatively modest incomes to cover their higher housing costs. This scheme was highly controversial and the mechanism for forcing councils to increase rents did not survive the Heath government, which lost the February 1974 general election. The national Rent Rebate scheme, however, did survive, and in any case the seeds had been planted for what was to become a persisting political division between Labour and the Conservatives. The former believed in keeping rent levels for council housing affordable to those in low-paid work without the need for additional means-tested benefit, while the Conservatives continued to favour personal rather than bricks-and-mortar subsidy. Most famously, Sir George Young, when Housing Minister in John Major's government, sought to reassure those, myself included, who argued against increasing rents for council and housing association tenancies, with the mantra that 'Housing Benefit will take the strain'.

There were respectable economic arguments on both sides. The Conservatives' case was that higher rents meant less need for government Social Housing Grant paid to social housing providers, and so allowed an expanded output, as the available levels of grant were spread more thinly. Indeed it was widely perceived that Sir George and his colleagues had craftily funded an expanded housing association programme in the early 1990s on the back of the DHSS's budget, as the inevitable consequence was a rise in Housing Benefit expenditure. The Labour case was not just a defence of the bricks-and-mortar subsidy regime that had made possible the large expansion in the council housing stock in the first three post-war decades. Labour also highlighted the problems, including the 'poverty trap', that were associated with extensive benefit dependency. We will return to this debate, but first need to cover the extraordinary story of how the Housing Benefit Scheme emerged from the two separate systems for helping tenants to meet housing costs (Supplementary Benefit, on the one hand, and Rent Rebates, on the other) that had been put in place by the 1970s.

The problem with having two separate schemes running in parallel was well summarised by Professor Peter Kemp.

> They were introduced and designed for a different purpose, one being concerned with income maintenance, the other with providing protection for rent increases. They had different means tests and were administered by different agencies under different government departments. The schemes had different structures and provided different levels of assistance. As a result, households with similar incomes, needs and housing costs could receive a different amount of assistance with their rent.[1]

This became known as the 'better-off' problem, with 400,000 households estimated in 1978 to be losing out through claiming the wrong benefit. It led to a recommendation from the Social Security Advisory Committee (SSAC) for a rationalisation that would bring the two schemes together into a single benefit, administered by local authorities rather than by the DHSS. The incoming Conservative government in 1979 seized on this as an opportunity to reduce government expenditure, but the scheme it introduced merely unified the administration while retaining different assessment frameworks. The mechanism proposed to address the 'better-off' problem was a top-up, called Housing Benefit Supplement, for those who would have been worse off if they were transferred from Supplement Benefit to Rent Rebates. But this involved a complex assessment and depended on effective transfers of documentation between DHSS offices and local authorities that would have tested the capability of even the most efficient organisations.

In the event, the scheme proved hugely problematic. Its implementation was marked by spectacular administrative failures, with vast piles of unprocessed files accumulating dust in council offices, and communications failure on a grand scale between the DHSS and local authorities. As co-author of the leading guide to the new Benefit scheme,[2] I was in heavy demand to offer training and consultancy services to local authorities throughout Britain and saw at first hand the extent of the problems. There were widespread and protracted delays in processing applications and making payments, extensive and often massive errors in calculating entitlements, almost universal confusion and serious alarm caused to tenants threatened with eviction as a consequence of not being able to pay their rent. Long queues formed outside local authority offices as those affected sought redress and, shamefully, in some areas people were simply turned away on the basis that the council did not have the capacity to deal with the numbers seeking resolution to their claims. *The Times* described it as 'the biggest administrative fiasco in the history of the Welfare State'.[3]

Although the government tried to minimise the chaos, describing it initially as teething difficulties, it soon had to acknowledge that the inherent complexity of the scheme made efficient administration almost impossible. Indeed the National Association of Citizens Advice Bureaux (NACAB) argued that the scheme in its then current form was unworkable.[4] Administration costs, originally estimated at £19 million, rocketed to £52.9 million in the first year.[5] Adding insult to injury, the government sought to make savings through introducing cuts to entitlement affecting over two million recipients. Not surprisingly, this provoked widespread public criticism, and the obvious failure of the new benefits scheme forced the government to announce a review within less than a year of its introduction. The review's conclusions, when published a year later, were unambiguous.

> Such an early review is an indication of the concern expressed at the complexities of the scheme and the difficulties experienced both by those claiming benefit and those responsible for its administration. It is clear to us that these difficulties can no longer be regarded as 'teething troubles' or as minor problems capable of solution by further amendments to the regulations. They run deeper than this and point to inherent flaws in the structure and scope of the scheme which no amount of tinkering or fine tuning will put right.[6]

The Review recommended a fundamental structural reform that would achieve the unification of the two separate benefit schemes, and most of the Review Team's recommendations were accepted and implemented by government. The new arrangements were brought into effect in April 1988, since when Housing Benefit has operated on a single-assessment system covering all claimants whether in or out of work and eliminating the 'better-off' problem. The scheme has continued on this same basis ever since, and while it has not been free of controversy this has reflected rising costs and changing attitudes to benefits as well as growing concern about the extent of fraud, rather than structural or administrative problems. Indeed the botched introduction in 1982–83 and the largely problem-free implementation of the 1988 scheme poses interesting questions of why government got its plans so wrong at the first time of asking. The answers are clear and straightforward:

1. over-hasty and insufficiently rigorous development of the policy, driven disproportionately by the DHSS's need to deliver savings, without adequate appraisal of whether the

original recommendations of the SSAC to deliver a unified benefit system were being achieved;

2. a serious gap between those developing the policy in DHSS, and those primarily charged with implementation (the local authorities). The problem was compounded by the cultural gaps, which we have already seen in relation to homelessness policy, between the two government departments primarily interested (DHSS and DoE). This was manifestly not a case of 'joined up' government;

3. inadequate challenge when the legislation (the 1982 Social Security and Housing Benefit Act) was progressing through Parliament;

4. an unrealistic implementation timetable for an inherently complex scheme. The legislation reached the statute book only in July 1982 and the regulations were issued only in August for a scheme that was due to start in November.

The fact that the 1988 reform was implemented with very little difficulty showed that lessons had been learned from the 1983 debacle. The review ensured a thorough appraisal of how the unification of two separate schemes was to be achieved. Local authorities were more closely involved in preparation for implementation, and had more time to commission and introduce the necessary computer programmes and administrative procedures, which were fundamental to efficient operation of a scheme affecting millions of recipients.

But if the administration of Housing Benefit had belatedly been put right, the scheme continued to arouse controversy. In the main, this reflected the continuing and apparently unstoppable rise in Housing Benefit expenditure. Table 3.1 sets out the growth both in numbers of recipients and in cost over the period from 1980/81 to the present.

As can be seen from Table 3.1, there has been an exponential rise in the cost of Housing Benefit over the 35 years since 1980. What had once been seen as a relatively small-scale supplement to meet the needs of a minority of people who could not otherwise afford their housing costs has been transformed into the main system for subsidising housing for all households in rented housing. Whereas the main subsidy in the early post-war period had been channelled to councils to enable them to build new housing that would then be let at significantly below market rents (rents that would be well within the means of most households in work), Housing Benefit increasingly came to support higher rent levels, approaching or at market levels. This, rather than a substantial and sustained increase in the number of recipients, is the explanation for the on-going rise in cost. As Table 3.1 illustrates, the total number of benefit recipients in 2015/16 is no greater than it was in 1985/86. Of course, the number of households receiving Housing Benefit has fluctuated, depending on wider economic and employment trends and on the benefit rules, which have been made more restrictive on several occasions during the period in question. But without the wider structural change in the nature of housing subsidy, these cyclical increases would not have translated into a continuing upward-only trajectory in cost.

Table 3.1: Housing Benefit take-up and cost, Great Britain

Year	1980/81	1985/86	1990/91	2000/01	2005/06	2010/11	2015/16
	Number of recipients (thousands)						
Rent rebates	2,843	3,710	2,922	2,230	1,753	1,502	1,344
Rent allowance	713	1,150	1,028	1,717	2,233	3,296	3,467
Total	**3,556**	**4,860**	**3,988**	**3,968**	**3,981**	**4,777**	**4,811**
	Cost (£ millions)						
Rent rebates	841	2,296	3,368	5,258	5,263	5,405	5,997
Rent allowance	183	881	1,799	5,904	8,666	16,022	18,371
Total	1,024	3,177	5,417	11,162	13,929	**21,427**	**24,367**
	Cost (£ millions, 2015/16 prices)						
Rent rebates	2,853	5,692	6,045	7,413	6,550	5,870	5,997
Rent allowance	621	2,184	3,208	8,324	10,786	17,400	18,371
Total	3,474	7,876	9,253	15,737	17,336	23,270	24,367

Source: Department for Work and Pensions, *Autumn Statement 2015 expenditure and caseload forecasts. UK Housing Review.*

There have been three principal trends driving the increase in Housing Benefit expenditure.

1. *Reduced council housing stock.* Whereas output of new council housing had been a major component in the total number of new homes built between the 1940s and 1970s, the supply of new council homes was progressively reduced through the 1980s and had been effectively brought to a standstill by the end of the 18-year period of Conservative government in 1997. This was a deliberate policy for a government that was committed to 'rolling back the frontiers of the State'. Not only was the tap of investment funding for new council housing closed down, but the existing stock of council housing was reduced in parallel, through the Right to Buy policy under which approaching two million homes were sold in England between 1980 and 2014.[7] So, the proportion of the country's housing accounted for by local authorities fell from 30% in 1980 to 7% in 2014. Tight restrictions on the use of the receipts from sales prevented councils from replacing sold units. As a consequence, by the late 1990s councils were able to accommodate only a reducing number of households in need.

   At the same time there was, as we saw in Chapter Two, a growing problem of disrepair in the remaining council housing stock, as the financial restrictions imposed by the government limited the scope for overdue maintenance, repairs and modernisation. This contributed to a growing interest in the possibility of transferring either all or part of a council's housing stock to housing associations that, through their ability to borrow on the private market, would be able to finance the renovation and on-going maintenance of the housing stock. Through this route a further very substantial part of the former council housing stock was transferred to other landlords, who, while still able to let at below market rent levels, were generally charging higher rents than were charged for council properties.

   So, with a smaller number of households in need finding accommodation through local authority housing, and with the alternative options generally charging higher rents, there was inevitable and on-going pressure for rising Housing Benefit expenditure.

2. *An expanded housing association role.* The origin of housing associations as voluntary, often charitable, organisations providing housing for people in need goes back a very long way, to medieval and Tudor times. Indeed many of the 'almshouses' that emerged from such initiatives are still with us today. In the 19th century, however, the role of housing associations developed as a number of wealthy industrialists sought to provide better-quality housing for their employees or established philanthropic associations to house working-class families who would otherwise be living in slums. Many of these associations, such as the Peabody Trust, are familiar names today. While their activities were eclipsed in the first half of the 20th century as local authorities became the major providers of new housing for the working classes, there was a renaissance in housing association activity in the 1960s and 1970s as the extent of unmet housing need in many urban and rural areas became evident. Indeed the need for an expanded voluntary sector input was recognised by both of the major political parties in the 1970s and this led to the unusually bipartisan 1974 Housing Act, opening up access to public finance for housing associations to supplement their private and philanthropic sources of income. The cross-party support for housing associations was partly a recognition that they were capable of meeting a number of specialist needs, such as housing for people needing care and support as well as a roof over their head, that were not necessarily catered for by local authority housing. It was also a recognition of the importance of providing an alternative to what otherwise was developing into a near-monopoly social housing sector.

During the 1980s, as council housing programmes were contracting, the Conservative government gave a further impetus to the expansion of housing associations by agreeing a framework for matching public sector grants with private borrowing, without the latter counting as public expenditure. The corollary was an increase in rent levels to ensure that the private loans could be serviced, but, as we have already seen, ministers were adamant at this time that this should not cause concern, as 'Housing Benefit will take the strain'. The problem was that neither the DHSS, nor its successor, the Department for Work and Pensions, was committed to indefinitely taking the strain, and indeed they became increasingly alarmed at the exponential rise in Housing Benefit expenditure prompted by rising rents and an apparently open-ended subsidy framework.

Under the 1997 Labour government a rent harmonisation scheme was put in place that obliged housing associations to set rents on the basis of a formula reflecting both the size and quality of the property and the local wage rates. This was designed to ensure both that rents were genuinely affordable to people in modestly paid work and that there was a coherent relationship between housing association and council rent levels. The policy was announced in the 2000 Housing Green Paper (covered more fully in Chapter Four) and operated successfully through the first decade of the 21st century. Social Housing Grant for new housing association developments allowed for rents to be set at levels within the criteria of the rent harmonisation scheme. However, in the opening Budget of the Coalition government the social housing budget was cut by more than 60% and the consequence was the abandonment of the rent harmonisation programme. Instead, the so-called 'affordable rent' regime was introduced, to require housing associations to increase rent levels in order to plug the hole left by the drastic cut in Social Housing Grant. Not only was this to apply to new developments; associations were also encouraged to transfer from the former social rent level to the higher affordable rent when existing properties came to be re-let. The outcome, when around two-thirds of housing association tenants were already in receipt of Housing Benefit, was a further hike in benefit expenditure. As can be seen from Table 3.2, between 2010 and 2015 the number of housing association tenants receiving Housing Benefit rose by just 5%, but the cost in real terms rose by 18%. This was in marked contrast to the previous decade, when the rent harmonisation policy had been in force, when the increase in the cost of Housing Benefit (+85%) was less than the increase in the number of housing association tenants receiving benefit (+91%).

Alarmed by the continuing rise in the cost of Housing Benefit, the incoming Conservative government in 2015 began a partial change of direction. It is now requiring housing associations to plan on the basis of a 1% annual reduction in rents. While this may have the effect of modifying the scale of increases in Housing Benefit, it does so at the expense of new investment, for rental income is crucial to the ability of associations to raise private finance to support new developments. And with continuing transfers from social rent tenancies to the so-called affordable rent tenure, there will be continuing upward pressure on Housing Benefit. In addition to the trends in council and housing association lettings, there has been a third and even more significant pressure in the same direction.

3. *Increased private renting.* At the beginning of the 20th century, around 90% of the population rented their homes privately. Yet, by 1990 the private rented sector had declined to a largely stigmatised rump tenure accounting for less than 10% of all homes in England. This remarkable change is ultimately attributable to three main factors. On the negative side, rent controls introduced in the First World War to counter profiteering and industrial unrest, and maintained in one form or another until 1988, gave landlords no incentive to invest in new or improved homes to rent. The outcome was a declining sector with worsening conditions. The problem was compounded by the highly publicised harassment and exploitation of vulnerable tenants by landlords such as Peter Rachman, whose name became synonymous with abuse. This reinforced the stigmatisation of private rented housing in the 1960s and 1970s. By contrast, the two 'growth' tenures of the 20th century, owner-occupation and council renting, both expanded massively, so that by 1980 they accounted for approaching 90% of all homes in England. They were the tenures of choice, whereas private renting was generally seen as a tenure of last resort, only for those who could not access better options.

In 1988 the Thatcher government legislated to remove rent controls and the associated security of tenure from new private lettings, but the expected recovery in the market was very slow in coming. As shadow Housing Minister in the 1990s, I was conscious of widespread concern among potential investors in private rented housing that an incoming Labour government would reintroduce rent controls, and this was a serious bar to recovery. Accordingly I gave several public commitments that Labour, while concerned to raise standards in a sector that was characterised by widespread disrepair, and committed to regulatory oversight of the worst-condition lodging houses (or Houses in Multiple Occupation – HMOs), would not reintroduce general rent controls. Even so, it was only in the early 2000s and following confirmation that the commitment would be honoured, explicitly set out in the 2000 Housing Green Paper,[8] that a strong recovery in investment in private renting took hold. But this was predominantly dependent on the growth of 'Buy to Let' investment rather than through an increased interest on the part of major institutional investors.

A reviving private rented sector did inevitably have significant implications for Housing Benefit. Not only were there more private tenants claiming Housing Benefit, but the rent levels were generally much higher than the rents charged by social landlords. As the way Housing Benefit is assessed reflects the actual rent level paid by the tenant, up to a maximum limit, any significant increase in the number of tenants living in higher-rent accommodation inevitably feeds through into higher benefit costs. So, Housing Benefit expenditure on Rent Allowance for private tenants rose dramatically, as can be seen from Table 3.2, in the first decade of the 21st century. Indeed it has continued to increase, despite the various measures adopted by the Coalition and now the Conservative government in its apparently desperate, and in many respects incoherent, attempts to contain Housing Benefit expenditure.

The government's rhetoric about benefits tends to stigmatise those on welfare, in contrast to those in work. However, one of the telling changes in benefit receipt in recent years has been the increasing number of those in work having to claim Housing Benefit to meet part of their housing costs. Whereas Beveridge had built his National Assistance scheme for help with housing

Table 3.2: Rent allowance recipients and cost

	1995	2000	2005	2010	2015
Housing associations					
No. of recipients (000s)	649	945	1,416	1,804	1,904
% of all housing association tenants	64%	65%	67%	70%	68%
Cost (£ million)	1,641	3,053	4,950	7,350	9,432
Cost (£ million 2015/16 prices)	2,572	4,304	6,160	7,982	9,432
Private tenants					
No. of recipients (000s)	1,168	771	817	1,492	1,563
% of all private tenants	52%	33%	27%	34%	29%
Cost (£ million)	3,804	2,851	3,716	8,672	8,939
Cost (£ million 2015/16 prices)	5,965	4,019	4,625	9,418	8,939

Note: Stock figures for 2015 are estimates.

Source: Department for Work and Pensions, *Autumn Statement 2015 expenditure and caseload forecasts. UK Housing Review*, Table 17d.

costs on the assumption that this would be needed to help only those temporarily out of the labour market, it was clear by the late 1990s that a growing proportion of households in regular employment needed Housing Benefit to cover their rent. This reflected the growing prevalence of low-paid jobs and was only marginally countered by the introduction of a minimum wage. Without substantial increases in income levels, the dependence of the low-paid on Housing Benefit to meet part of their rent is likely to continue, particularly in areas with high housing costs such as London and South East England. In these areas even those on average wage levels face real difficulty in meeting market rents, so the availability of Housing Benefit is likely to remain a key issue for many people in middle- to low-paid jobs looking for a private tenancy. This could become a very serious issue in the coming years because the inadequate supply of social rented homes makes increased dependency on private lettings inevitable. Against this background it is difficult to see how further increases in Housing Benefit expenditure can be avoided, other than through deeper cuts in benefit entitlement for individual recipients.

A further irony is that the burgeoning cost of Housing Benefit has not been matched by a rising trend in housing supply. On the contrary, as a comparison of Table 3.2 with Figure 4.1 in the next chapter demonstrates, the rise in Housing Benefit expenditure to unprecedented levels in the second decade of the 21st century has coincided with the lowest-recorded peace-time output of new homes. This has, not surprisingly, led to questions posed most powerfully by the IPPR (Institute for Public Policy Research)[9] as to whether we should as a matter of policy seek to reverse the trend in housing subsidy so as to promote more direct capital investment in new and improved homes. This case for a switch in housing subsidy from 'benefit to bricks' has an obvious superficial attraction. But it is not the case that we can simply reverse the clock by switching spending back to investment subsidy rather than Housing Benefit. Any such process would have to be managed in a highly sensitive way so as to avoid the obvious threat posed to the living standards and, indeed, continued occupation of their homes of around five million households currently dependent on Housing Benefit. There is also the important consideration that the lending institutions that support in particular the housing association investment programme take considerable comfort from the availability of Housing Benefit to support the rent payments of tenants who might otherwise be unable to meet their housing costs. Any serious threat to the on-going availability of Housing Benefit would have a damaging impact on investor confidence and, therefore, the ability of housing associations to raise the private finance that meets the overwhelming majority of their capital investment programme. That, in turn, would adversely impact on the number of homes they could hope to develop.

The IPPR's report recognised the significant obstacles that would need to be overcome in order to effect such a switch from benefits to bricks, and the need for careful handling of the process. It suggested that this would be best achieved by devolving Housing Benefit and housing investment budgets from central to local government, leaving it to individual local authorities to determine how to split the available total capital investment and benefit. It is, however, difficult to see this working successfully, with most local authorities lacking the scale, capacity and expertise to manage all the complex strands involved in determining how to allocate their total resource in the most efficient and cost-effective way. Given that housing markets generally cover a much wider area than that contained within any one local authority boundary, there is in any case a strong argument for approaching the challenge more strategically and across broader areas.

However, the underlying insight of the IPPR's report is the need to recognise the interdependence of policies affecting housing investment and benefits. While decisions continue to be made with little apparent concern for the wider consequences, as with the imposition of the 1% annual rent reduction on housing associations, there will inevitably be incoherent policy outcomes. Breaking down the silos so as to allow a better-integrated framework for decision making on both benefits and investment would appear to have considerable potential benefits, in just the same way as achieving a better-integrated approach to planning social care and health provision. Against the background of potential devolution to combined authorities in city regions such as Greater Manchester (see Chapter Seven), there might be an opportunity to explore the scope for integrating policy making on Housing Benefit and housing investment. In London, where the mayor, rather than the 32 borough councils, has controlled the housing capital investment budget since it was devolved from the Homes and Communities Agency, a similar opportunity could be available. This oversight of an area containing approaching nine million inhabitants facilitates strategic decision making where investment can be targeted to best effect. It is possible to envisage a shift in emphasis between investment and benefits expenditure being achieved over a period of time, but this will require substantial additional capital funding in order to increase the supply of homes available to rent at social rent levels.

There are no easy and simple solutions. As in many other comparable policy areas, the issues that have to be addressed are complex, and in some respects intractable. But underlying this web of complications there is a simple question that needs to be posed as the starting point for any new policy formulation. That is, 'How can we most effectively generate a supply of homes sufficient to meet the needs of society, and do so in a way that enables the residents to meet the costs of that housing?' We are currently a long way from achieving a satisfactory answer to that question. How we might begin to develop a credible response is the subject of the next chapter.

FOUR

Why can't we build enough homes?

Figure 4.1 is the most famous graph in all analyses of housing supply in England. It shows the total number of homes built in each year between 1946 and 2014 and the tenure breakdown. The headline stories are obvious.

Figure 4.1: House-building by tenure, England, 1946–2014

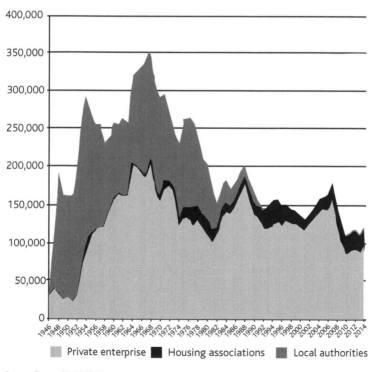

Source: Barnes, Y. (2015) 'A city village approach to regenerating housing estates', in A. Adonis and B. Davies *City villages: Better communities*, IPPR. Data from DCLG live tables.

1. An exceptionally high level of output through most of the 1950s, 1960s and 1970s, prompted by the need to make good war-time losses and shortages, as well as an ambitious slum-clearance programme. New provision depended overwhelmingly on the two post-war growth tenures, owner-occupation and council renting.

2. A lower output of around 150,000 homes a year on average through the 1980s, 1990s and 2000s, but with a significantly different tenure breakdown. Owner-occupation cements its place as the dominant tenure, new council output declines to almost nothing, while housing associations emerge as substantial providers of social rented housing, but not on the scale that councils had previously met. At the end of this period private renting is once again growing and will soon overtake the social-housing landlords as the largest source of rented homes, but this comes largely through conversion from other tenures rather than from the purposeful construction of new homes to rent privately.

3. A further serious decline in output following the financial crisis of 2008, with a slow recovery still leaving output in 2015 below the pre-2008 levels. Owner-occupation remains the lead tenure, albeit at a reduced level, while housing associations continue as the main source of social rented housing and the growth of private renting is sustained.

Over-simplistic responses to the evidence in Figure 4.1 imply that we should, as a matter of policy, seek to return to the model of the initial post-war years to remedy the current shortfall and ensure a good supply of affordable homes to rent. While this is an entirely understandable reaction to the obviously inadequate current output of new homes, it is neither a practical nor a desirable policy response. It is impractical because local authorities do not have the capacity to deliver a housing programme on that scale, and it is undesirable because it would mean that we had failed to learn lessons from the adverse consequences of that post-war building boom. In the pursuit of quantity, with ministers from both main political parties vying to out-build their predecessors (Macmillan achieving 300,000 in the 1950s, Wilson 400,000 in the 1960s – in each case across the whole of Great Britain), we too often lost sight of the importance of quality and community. Many of the homes built in that era were poorly designed and badly built and, as a result, proved unsustainable. The problem was compounded by poor management of the council housing stock in several areas, which allowed many estates to deteriorate faster than would otherwise have occurred. Political pressures to minimise rent increases, particularly when elections were due, also contributed to under-investment in the maintenance of the council housing stock. A combination of poor design, construction defects and unsatisfactory management and maintenance led to the physical decline and stigmatisation of substantial numbers of council estates. So, by the 1980s and 1990s too many of the homes that had been built over the previous three or four decades as a solution to the country's post-war housing shortage had been transformed into part of the on-going problem.

That doesn't just apply to substandard council estates that subsequently had to be demolished or radically regenerated. Much of the private housing of that era was built to very poor energy-efficiency standards and now requires expensive retrofitting to reduce emissions and fuel costs. Also, the patterns of private housing development in that era often involved profligate use of land and created settlements at too low a density to sustain community facilities such as local shops and public transport services. So, while we do need to expand output, we must never lose sight of the importance of good design and place-making as well as high-quality construction to ensure that the homes and communities we build are good places to live and leave a lasting legacy. We certainly do not need to sacrifice quality to quantity, and the scale of building required, estimated by most experts at between 220,000 and 230,000 new homes a year,[1] is not so large as to make us lose sight of other considerations. Indeed it is significantly below the levels of housebuilding seen in the 1950s, 1960s and 1970s.

One strange feature of housing history is that at that very point in time when we were building most homes, we were also imposing a pattern of tenure segregation that was socially disastrous. Almost all the new homes built in that era were either for owner-occupation or for council renting, yet rarely if ever were they built on the same site. Not only did this lead to stigmatised 'sink' estates, and dormitory suburbs with a density too low to sustain local shops and community facilities, but it is strikingly at variance with the way people have lived for thousands of years. Look at the pattern of housing in medieval, Tudor or Georgian times, and you will find rich and poor living not just in the same street, but often in the same house. Of course, wealthier people enjoyed much grander and more comfortable accommodation, and within the house 'upstairs' and 'downstairs' were clearly delineated, but the idea that people with different income levels should live in entirely separate areas didn't take hold until much later.

The rapid expansion of the economy in the Victorian era did lead to increased social segregation, with often poor-quality housing for the new industrial working class being put up in haste and with little thought for health or amenity. However, there were other forces at work. The expanding urban middle class depended on domestic servants to maintain their life-style, and this to a significant degree countered the other pressures leading towards different classes living in different areas. Despite various moves towards deliberate social segregation of housing in the first half of the 20th century, of which the notorious Cutteslowe Walls in Oxford[2] provide perhaps the starkest example, it was only in the second half of the 20th century that this became the default pattern of development. It turned out to be a very unhappy experiment, starkly at odds with the vision of the minister who initiated the post-war house-building programme, Nye Bevan, who spoke eloquently of replicating the rich tapestry of traditional English and Welsh villages where the doctor, the grocer, the butcher and the labourer all live side by side.[3]

While the changed pattern of provision in the 1980s reflected political choices by the Conservative government to reduce investment in council housing, there were other influences at work. From the late 1960s it had been recognised that too much emphasis had been given to slum clearance and insufficient thought to the scope for renovation and improvement of existing homes. Indeed the need for new building at the time was partly the product of extensive clearance, to replace demolished homes that might in other circumstances have had a continued use. There was also a growing awareness of the disruptive social impacts of large-scale clearance and rehousing programmes.[4] Whereas in the immediate post-war era a culture of deference to authority still prevailed, by the 1960s the assumption that decisions taken by government and local government would generally be sound and should be accepted without question was increasingly being challenged. The re-emergence of housing associations at this time as significant providers of social housing partly reflected the work that they had been pioneering in many urban areas, improving and renovating existing properties to provide decent homes for families in need. The bi-partisan support for an expanded role for housing associations under the 1974 Housing Act reflected both a recognition of the need for this work and a desire for greater diversity in the provision of social rented housing; for the rapid expansion of council housing had in some areas created large near-monopolies of rented housing, not always managed in ways that showed sensitivity to the concerns of tenants and prospective tenants.

So, there was a growing consensus in the 1990s on the need for a more pluralistic framework for social housing, embracing councils, housing associations and a small but enthusiastic self-management sector comprising co-ops and tenant-management organisations. There was also support for mixed-tenure development, giving opportunities for people on different income levels to live side by side in good-quality homes not differentiated by walls, gates or 'poor doors'. When I became Housing Minister in 1999, these were some of the themes I was particularly keen to promote. However, the key challenge was the large backlog of substandard council housing.

The English House Condition Survey of 1996 had put a £10 billion price tag on the programme needed to tackle the problem of substandard council housing. This by itself was an indication of the scale of the problem, but it proved to be a serious under-estimate of the investment needed to bring the whole stock of council-owned homes up to modern standards. By the time the Decent Homes Programme, the Labour government's response to the challenge, had run its course the total cost had reached almost £40 billion. With the total provision for housing capital investment inherited from the Major government in 1997 at just over £3 billion, as illustrated in Table 4.1, and this having to cover all sectors including private sector grants and housing association development as well as local authority spending, it was clearly impossible to achieve the necessary outcome without both a longish time frame and substantial additional private investment to complement public sector funding. The Decent Homes Programme recognised this with a 10-year implementation period and four funding strands to incentivise diversity and high standards. In addition to the funding available for direct council investment, three further options were promoted, including Arm's Length Management Organisations (ALMOs), separate entities owned by the authority but with operational independence, and stock transfer to housing associations that would also be able to access additional private funding. By the end of the 10-year period more than two million homes had been transformed, most benefitting from new windows, kitchens, bathrooms and, in some cases, roofs, as well as wider environmental improvements and better insulation to improve thermal efficiency. This was probably the most important outcome of the 2000 Housing Green Paper that set out the Labour government's plans to tackle the country's housing needs.

A second strand in that Green Paper was the importance of making services to social housing tenants more responsive to their needs and aspirations. There were a number of different elements proposed, including a new choice-based allocations system to allow prospective tenants more say in where they lived; a rent-harmonisation programme (already referred to in Chapter Three) to reduce discrepancies and anomalies between rents charged by councils and housing associations; and a strong focus on promoting mixed communities where tenants and owners could live side by side. I had the good fortune of being able to promote the mixed-communities agenda through Greenwich Millennium Village in my Greenwich and Woolwich parliamentary constituency. GMV was the first in a programme launched by John Prescott in 1997 to encourage the development of exemplary new housing schemes with a strong focus on meeting high design and environmental standards and with the aim of building communities rather than housing estates. On a formerly heavily polluted ex-industrial site, Ralph Erskine's plan has delivered well-designed, high-quality homes for sale or rent, and with intermediate tenure options, pepper-potted so as to achieve tenure blindness, set in an attractive landscape, with a good local school, health and shopping facilities, excellent public transport links, and with a strong focus on environmental performance. GMV has been widely recognised as a model for new sustainable residential developments.[5]

The Green Paper also focused on improving standards and options in the private rented sector, introducing a tenancy deposit scheme to safeguard tenants' funds and reduce the incidence of conflict between landlord and tenant, promoting local accreditation schemes to encourage and support small landlords and introducing a selective licensing scheme to allow local authorities to take more effective action against exploitation and abuse, particularly in Houses in Multiple Occupation (HMOs).

In Chapter Two I have already referred to the changes in homelessness policy introduced following the Green Paper, including an extension in the groups to be treated as in priority need and a stronger focus on prevention and support services. Legislation to give effect to these policies was introduced before the 2001 general election, but only passed into law in 2002 when Charlie Falconer had taken over from me as Housing Minister. The Green Paper also gave considerable attention to a range of policies designed to promote and support sustainable homeownership. These included new opportunities for middle income households to access homeownership, and better-focused measures to assist low-income households to maintain and improve their homes and to tackle the problems of abandonment and the collapse of market confidence in areas of low demand. The Green Paper also included the government's plans to extend leaseholders' rights and to introduce a new Commonhold tenure so as to enable those living in flats and apartments to own their block collectively, and measures to improve standards through the Building Regulations and to streamline the house buying and selling process. I will return to some of these issues in the next chapter.

In summary, the Green Paper was the most comprehensive overview of housing policy for almost a quarter of a century and launched or promoted many programmes and initiatives that had a significant influence over the following years. A great deal of credit should go to the civil service team led by Michael Gahagan that was responsible for its drafting. While the impact of many of these policies, such as the Decent Homes Programme, was generally very positive, the criticism that can be levelled at the Green Paper, particularly with the benefit of hindsight, is that it did not give sufficient emphasis to the need to expand housing output. We are now acutely aware of the problems, not least of access and affordability, caused by the chronic shortage of homes. But back in the late 1990s, when the Green Paper was being drafted, the climate of opinion was very different. I have already referred to the problem of abandonment and the collapse of market confidence in many areas, particularly in the Midlands and North of England. Expanding the supply of new homes was clearly not appropriate in or around such areas. Indeed there was a lively debate about the need to restrain new house building on greenfield sites in order to promote urban regeneration, as well as to safeguard the countryside from profligate and unsustainable development.

The Urban Taskforce, chaired by Richard Rogers,[6] had given a strong impetus to this approach and helped the government achieve a remarkable increase in the proportion of new housing developed on brownfield sites, up from 55% to over 70%[7] in the first years of the 21st century. Of course it was recognised that different pressures applied in London and much of the South East, and that there had to be higher levels of house building in areas where supply was lagging behind new household formation. But it is important to remember that London's population had only recently begun to recover from half a century of decline and the speed and scale of the growth that was to occur in the 21st century was not anticipated. Outside London in the wider South East the main obstacle then, as still today, was the resistance of many councils and communities to new housing development in their areas. At the time, many of us involved in government and in the housing sector believed, perhaps naively, that these nimby tendencies could over time be countered by determined advocacy focusing on four key themes.

1. The 'brownfield first' presumption, together with the emphasis on more sustainable densities in new housing schemes, both

clearly set out in Planning Policy Guidance Note 3 (PPG3),[8] would, it was hoped, reassure the public that much greater efforts were being made to ensure that previously developed land would, wherever possible, be the first choice for new housing, and counter the preference of many house-builders for profligate use of greenfield sites.

2. Increased capital investment from 2000 onwards (Table 4.1), together with the emphasis in PPG3 on mixed-tenure developments, including an appropriate element of affordable housing, would also provide reassurance that local needs for affordable housing would be met as an integral part of new developments.

3. The strong focus on improving the design and quality of new housing developments, and the promotion of exemplary new schemes, such as GMV to which I have already referred, would, it was hoped, counter the widely held view that new housing developments tended to be 'blots on the landscape' rather than enhancing the attractiveness of the area.

4. The objective evidence of increasing need for new homes in many areas, reinforced by examinations in public in the course of the planning process, would eventually moderate if not totally overcome the resistance of nimby-dominated councils that were reluctant to make adequate provision for housing in their local plans.

There were also good grounds for believing that housing output could be expanded progressively, with an increased social and affordable housing programme complementing the activities

Table 4.1: Gross housing capital investment England (£ million)

Year	1997/98	1998/99	1999/20	2000/01	2001/02	2002/03	2003/04	2004/05
Total	3137	3224	3127	3582	3885	4749	5303	5641
ADP	702	621	638	717	775	921	1818	1654

2005/6	2006/7	2007/08	2008/09	2009/10	2010/11	2011/12	2012/13	2013/14
6133	6458	7071	7513	8278	6572	4744	4244	4423
1599	1951	2063	2612	3764	2509	1470	982	651

Source: CCHPR, *UK Housing Review 2015*, Table 62a.

of private house-builders. Increased provision for government housing investment was initially heavily concentrated on the Decent Homes Programme because of the overriding priority of transforming the condition of the social housing stock, but by the mid-2000s, as Table 4.1 shows, the Housing Corporation's Approved Development Programme (ADP), mainly supporting new housing association development, was also increasing substantially. The combination of grant funding from the Housing Corporation, later the Homes and Community Agency, with private borrowing by housing associations and contributions either in cash or in kind under Section 106 (S. 106) agreements with private developers, made possible a significantly larger programme than could be funded solely by public spending. While the S. 106 mechanism had been in place since the early 1990s, it had not been used to the extent that was both feasible and desirable. Hence the encouragement to local authorities to make greater use of the process in PPG3, issued in 1998.

The added advantage of increasing the number of social and affordable homes on sites being developed by private house-builders was its contribution to the mixed communities agenda. The assumption that housing output could be expanded through these routes appeared to be working, as can be seen from both Figures 4.1 and 4.2, which demonstrate a steady rise in the completion of new homes through the first decade of the 21st century, until the 2008 financial crisis. Indeed, as Figure 4.2 shows, the continued availability of government grant allowed the social and affordable housing programme to be sustained through to 2010/11 even when the level of homes generated through S. 106 obligations fell in the aftermath of the credit crunch. The value of such counter-cyclical public sector investment cannot be over-emphasised. Indeed the availability of 'Kickstart' and other public investment programmes deployed in 2009–10, when John Healey was Housing Minister and Sir Bob, now Lord Kerslake, headed the Homes and Communities Agency (HCA), not only ensured the continuation of some house building in the exceptionally bleak financial climate post 2008 but also helped to avert potential bankruptcies among some of the larger house-building businesses that were severely hit by the downturn. Of course the credit crunch did have a very serious adverse impact

Figure 4.2: Affordable housing completions in England, 2004/05 to 2012/13

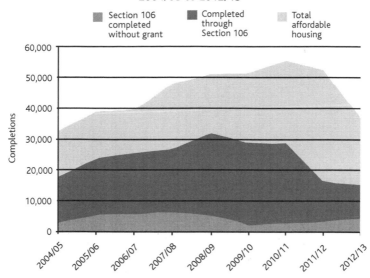

Source: DCLG live tables and HCA, printed in TCPA *Journal*, November 2015.

on housing supply, but it is not the case, as the Conservatives have tried to claim subsequently, that the Labour government failed to increase house building. As the Department for Communities and Local Government's (DCLG) own figures show, net additions to the housing stock showed sustained improvements through the years up to 2007, in which year they totalled over 207,000, within touching distance of the level necessary to match new household formation.[9] Even including the years of recession, the Labour government's average annual output of new homes was 35,000 a year more than what the Coalition government achieved in the following five years, 2010 to 2015.

While in my view it was feasible to achieve a sustained increase in housing output on the basis set out in points 1 to 4 above (pages 60–61), there were other voices in government who believed that a more far-reaching reform of the planning system was necessary. This is one of the leitmotifs that have run through debates on planning for many decades. As a result, we have seen repeated so-called 'reforms' of the planning system in Britain, all of which have proved controversial and none of which can be said to have wholly delivered the promised improvements. I was sceptical of the case for the introduction by the Labour government of the Regional Spatial Strategies (RSS) framework in the early years of the 21st century. Indeed I suspect that it was my known reluctance to undertake a major restructuring of the planning system, with all the consequent upheavals, controversy and disruption that helps explain why, in 2001, I was moved from the Housing and Planning brief that I had held for just two years to a different portfolio (Local and Regional Government) in the same department. My reluctance was not based on any great love for the 1980s planning regime that we inherited from the Conservatives. It had its weaknesses. But so too did the RSS framework, and so too does the National Planning Policy Framework (NPPF) introduced by the Coalition government after 2010. Any fundamental change to the system inevitably causes a period of uncertainty in which it is difficult to plan with any confidence. The disruption caused in the short term is only justifiable if there is a real prospect of substantial long-term benefits, but, given the nature of the planning system, this is difficult if not impossible to guarantee, as I will now explain.

The planning system has to mediate between conflicting pressures and interests and, ultimately, to deliver judgements on the respective benefits and disadvantages of particular development options. Those primarily interested in the economic benefits likely to flow from development generally see planning as a serious obstacle to growth and resent the regulatory burden it imposes on business. This point of view has for some time been supported by elements in the Treasury who believe that planning has acted as a brake on productivity and economic growth in Britain. Conversely, those most interested in promoting or defending the ability of local communities to shape their own areas and those concerned about the adverse environmental impacts of development argue for a planning system that allows maximum discretion to local councils, and object to targets imposed by national or regional policy makers and to the ability of developers to appeal against a local decision to refuse planning consent. Whatever system is adopted has to find a balance between those competing tensions. A failure to find such a balance carries the serious risk of undermining public confidence in the ability of the planning system to achieve fair and reasonable outcomes, and so opens the door, as the history of road-building schemes in the 1980s and 1990s demonstrates, to the advocates of direct action to stop or delay unwelcome schemes. Despite the experience of Twyford Down, the Newbury by-pass and other controversial sites, the Treasury ideologues find it difficult to recognise that shifting the balance in the planning system is not an easy path to growth and productivity, but an open door to another generation of 'swampies'. Calibrating the balance so as to deliver the optimum outcome is not easy at any time. But it is particularly difficult in a period of rapid change when all the balls are up in the air and it is far from clear where each will land. Uncertainty in the planning system is seen as highly undesirable by almost all parties. Developers repeatedly emphasise the need for certainty if they are to attract investment, while environmentalists are particularly alarmed by the prospect of opportunistic grabs for sites that in their view should be protected.

The way that the NPPF came into being and reached its current form is a very instructive story. In opposition, the Conservatives had strongly criticised the RSS framework, which they claimed resulted in the imposition of unreasonable 'top-down' requirements on local councils by central or regional bodies. This, they claimed, fuelled an anti-development reaction. In its place they argued for a 'localist' approach and, following the 2010 General Election, they set about dismantling RSSs with unseemly haste. Indeed they appeared obsessed with the need to abolish the system they inherited before having a clear view of what should replace it. The emphasis was on promoting neighbourhood planning, which has merit as a means of engaging local communities in some areas, but cannot substitute for strategic planning. Most communities that have engaged in neighbourhood planning are keen to preserve the existing character of the area. Indeed many of those involved have come disproportionately from better-off sections of the population. It would be unrealistic to expect such groups to advocate changes designed to promote social justice and expand the supply of homes to meet the needs of the least advantaged in society. That having been said, the promotion of neighbourhood planning would have been unobjectionable had it not been accompanied by the abolition of RSSs, leaving no mechanism for linking national estimates of housing need with local provision. In its absence there is no way of ensuring that the sum of local decisions adds up to the total national requirement. The whole approach was predicated on the heroic assumption that, freed of the 'shackles' of 'top-down' obligations, local communities would do the right thing and ensure that enough homes were built in their area, as well as magically contributing sufficient numbers to meet national requirements.

In the event, local reactions were very different. The not insubstantial number of people opposed to development in most areas of the country took heart and urged their councils to seize the opportunity both to reject unwelcome planning applications and to resist pressure for increased provision for new homes in local plans. The main house-building companies were, not surprisingly, alarmed and turned to their allies in the Treasury, who before long weighed in to the argument, insisting on a policy volte-face. This in turn led, predictably, to calls of betrayal by those bodies, including the National Trust and the Campaign for the Protection of Rural England, that had been led to believe that the promised 'localist' framework would give more scope to local communities to say 'No' to unwelcome development. After two years of bad-tempered wrangling between the parties, described subsequently by one Conservative MP as reflecting the respective Jekyll and Hyde faces of the government,[10] a compromise NPPF was produced that included a presumption in favour of 'sustainable development' but that avoided including any working definition of what that meant. In consequence, lawyers are having a field day and ever more cases are being determined on appeal. While the level of planning consents for housing has now increased, the output of new homes remains substantially below what was being achieved under the old RSS framework in the years immediately before the credit crunch. It is therefore difficult to avoid the conclusion that 'reform' of the planning system is not necessarily, as some commentators claim, the key to increasing the level of house building. There are a number of other factors at work.

As Figure 4.1 makes clear, private house-builders have rarely exceeded an output of 150,000 new homes a year in England. This is partly a reflection of their business model, which gives greater importance to profitability than to volume. Indeed there is a curious paradox in a situation where, over the post-recession period, house-builders have recorded dramatic increases in their profitability at a time when output of new homes has been at historically low levels. It was estimated in 2013 that the stock market valuation of Britain's largest house-builders had risen over the previous five years by 342%, while their output of new homes had marginally declined over the same period.[11] The shortage of homes has of course helped to inflate house prices, even at a time when affordability problems have made it hard for many potential buyers to afford a home. It would certainly not be in the interests of house-builders to see the market flooded with new homes, prompting a fall in house prices. While it is certainly reasonable to expect some further growth in the number of new homes built for sale by private house-builders, this is unlikely to generate more than 150,000 homes a year. This is all the more probable given the dramatic decline in the number of small and medium-sized builders (SMEs), who traditionally accounted for a significant proportion of total housing output. In 2008, SME builders were responsible for 44,000 new home completions. By 2015 this had more than halved, to just 18,000. Indeed the number of SME-registered builders has reduced by three-quarters over the 25 years since 1990, and there is little sign of a recovery in this sector.

So, if we are to meet the level of new house building seen by most experts as necessary to match need, we will have to find an additional 80,000 homes from other sources. From the late 1940s to the 1970s council housing provided this volume or more, but, as I have already argued, it would be unwise to try to resurrect a large mono-tenure public housing development programme. Instead we need to be encouraging a more pluralist programme of new homes designed to meet a range of economic circumstances, including social rented housing at rents within the means of those in low-paid work, and intermediate rented homes with rents pitched between those applying to social-rented tenancies and market rents. Additionally, we need continued expansion in the provision of good-quality private rented homes at market rents, with, hopefully, a growing proportion of these generated by institutional investment.

A range of low-cost homeownership options should also be part of the package, catering for the needs of those on middle incomes who cannot afford outright owner-occupation but who could support the costs of a shared-ownership lease, shared equity, discounted market sale or other form of below-market housing for sale. Many of the models that have been developed over recent years to facilitate homeownership at below market costs ensure that the benefit remains available to future generations. The Pocket model, for example, enables buyers to acquire the full ownership of their home at around 20% below market value, and ensures that the discount continues to be available to future buyers through a covenant requiring resale only to people with incomes below a set threshold. Such mechanisms are essential if the benefits of low-cost ownership schemes are not to be dissipated through windfall gains to the initial purchaser who acquires a home at a below-market value but can subsequently sell on the open market. That, regrettably, is the basis of the current Conservative government's 'starter home' scheme, which proposed that the initial beneficiaries should be able to cash in after just five years. This has all the hallmarks of a scheme designed for the short term and pandering to self-interest, rather than delivering long-term benefits to future generations. It has the added disadvantage of being a policy that emerged from political calculation without any credible evidence base, shortly before a general election.

As well as a range of different tenure options, we need a variety of providers. This is not just to avoid a return to the patterns of the past in which monopoly provision thrived and where too often the quality of service to the public suffered in consequence, but also to reflect the variety of different models of, for example, intermediate rented and low-cost homeownership housing currently available, and the likelihood of new models emerging in the future. Encouraging innovative new entrants into the market is a powerful safeguard against complacency and against the market's being dominated by small numbers of relatively large players. In the case of both private house-builders and housing associations, we have seen a growing concentration of power in the hands of a small number of organisations and a significant decline in the influence of SMEs. Countering the tendencies towards the development of oligopolies, and promoting a more pluralist framework for the provision of different types of tenure makes economic sense and should also protect the interests of the public. It would also go with the grain of today's market, where there is growing interest in the possibility of self-build and custom-build solutions.

One further option needs to be promoted as part of the package necessary to deliver at least 80,000 homes a year in addition to those likely to be built by the private house-building industry. Throughout the immediate post-war period, from the 1940s to the 1980s, a substantial number of new towns were created and delivered a significant proportion of the new homes built in that period. In the early stages, the new towns were primarily building the equivalent of council homes, and indeed in most cases their housing stock was transferred to the local authority in their area when they were wound up. However, in the later stages new towns like Milton Keynes provided a range of housing for different tenures and needs. By attracting new industry and employment into the area and developing cultural and recreational opportunities, development corporations in places like Milton Keynes played a crucial place-making role in bringing an attractive and vibrant new city into existence. Given the particularly acute housing problems facing London and the South East, there is, in my view, an overwhelmingly powerful case for the designation of a new generation of new communities. Tentative steps have been taken over the past decade to promote 'Eco Towns' and 'Garden Cities', but to date they have made only a very modest impact, in no way matching either the scale of need or what was achieved between the 1940s and 1980s. Although most commentators accept the logic for establishing new settlements in appropriate locations, the politicians involved have invariably shied away when confronted by local resistance to any plans for new development in their area. Most spectacularly, Housing Minister Brandon Lewis rubbished the winning entry in a 2014 competition, promoted by the Conservative peer Lord Wolfson to encourage imaginative new Garden City proposals, within hours of the outcome's being announced, for fear that he and the government might be associated with a plan that involved some development in the Green Belt. The speed with which the Wolfson Prize winner was binned was also perhaps not unconnected with the location of the proposed development, in close proximity to the Prime Minister's Witney constituency.

Public opposition to development in the Green Belt is an entirely understandable reaction to the fear of a return to poorly designed development indiscriminately gobbling up the countryside. It was precisely the experience of such 'ribbon development' in the 1930s that fuelled the case for the designation of Green Belt areas in the aftermath of the Second World War. The purpose of Green Belt is to restrict urban sprawl, but most people think of it as a means of protecting beautiful landscape. They would be surprised to learn that the Green Belt, as currently defined, includes not just very unattractive scrubland sites but areas already under concrete such as Cambridge airport! The consequence of this confusion is that, as was seen with the Wolfson Prize fiasco, serious attempts to reconcile the need for new homes in areas that are currently landlocked with the protection of the wider countryside rarely if ever get beyond the stage of a headline denouncing the 'Green Belt under threat'.

If we are to meet housing needs better in South East England, there will have to be new settlements, yet current Green Belt designations make it very hard if not impossible to identify appropriate locations that would prove truly sustainable. We have to inject a better sense of realism into the debate about Green Belt. Yes, Green Belt is and must remain a strong safeguard against urban sprawl, but it must not become a straightjacket that prevents well-designed and sustainable developments from ever being considered in areas currently designated as Green Belt. Indeed the perverse consequence of current tight Green Belt designations around some expanding cities is to promote greater car dependency and unsustainable development patterns as people look for homes beyond the Green Belt but travel back to the city to work. Of course there are anxieties that a more flexible approach could open the door to indiscriminate and inappropriate developments in the Green Belt. That is why strong safeguards are essential, and proposals for adjustment to Green

Belt boundaries should be approved only following thorough and rigorous local plan reviews, and where the proposed development can be demonstrated to meet exacting sustainability standards and bring incontrovertible benefits. In my period as Planning Minister, I was prepared on certain occasions to approve developments within the Green Belt, but we were always clear on the need to maintain, and indeed expand, the area covered by Green Belt protection, so that the overarching objective to prevent indiscriminate urban sprawl was not compromised. I remain convinced that such an approach is essential if we are to achieve a more mature discourse on this highly sensitive subject.

So, a comprehensive approach to the expansion of housing supply is clearly required. The nearest that we have got to the development of such a plan in recent years was the Lyons Report,[12] published in autumn 2014. Sir Michael Lyons and his colleagues gave an impressive overview of the housing market and an indication of the approach most likely to deliver the necessary outcome. The Lyons Report recognised that there were no magic 'silver bullets' that could alone transform the supply of homes. Instead it recognised the need for a sustained programme of investment by the full range of organisations from both public and private sectors. Unfortunately, Sir Michael had been commissioned to do this work by the Labour Party, so any prospect of its adoption and implementation died with the general election of 2015. Instead of a comprehensive and evidence-based approach to housing and planning policy, the Conservative government opted for an ideologically driven approach with a strong focus on the promotion of homeownership and a further weakening of the already inadequate means of delivering social housing. While the government claimed that its overarching objective is to increase the output of new homes, it is difficult to see how its policies will deliver the step change necessary to raise output levels towards 230,000 a year. As we have seen, there are self-imposed limits on the number of new homes that house-builders will produce for the private market. Furthermore, the high price levels even for modest-sized homes for sale in most parts of southern England pose a serious obstacle to a high proportion of prospective buyers. Without a substantial level of social, affordable, intermediate and private rented housing the gap is very unlikely to close significantly. And without these types of provision, large numbers of people on modest and low incomes will have no effective means of paying for a home.

Yet a series of measures taken since the 2015 general election, including the introduction of a Right to Buy for housing association tenants, the powers to require councils to sell higher-value properties, a rent cap on housing associations and further cuts in Housing Benefit entitlement, together with a marked shift of emphasis in favour of owner-occupation at the expense of the provision of social and affordable homes, all have the effect of reducing the capacity of local authorities and housing associations to provide an expanded supply of homes. It is not an encouraging scenario. The likely consequence will be continued upward pressure on already seriously over-inflated house prices, which could in turn prompt a further crash and readjustment, with all the damaging impacts we saw in 2008.

In parallel, unsustainably high rent levels are likely to remain, putting further pressure on household budgets and Housing Benefit expenditure. The already inadequate supply of social rented housing will contract further through Right to Buy sales and the forced disposal of council housing in high-value areas. This will accentuate pressures towards social segregation as social rented housing disappears from high-value areas and those dependent on lower-rent accommodation have to move away. The spectre of polarisation in cities such as Paris, with an affluent centre ringed by stigmatised 'banlieues', could well become a reality in London, which to date has impressively managed to avoid such an outcome. While other cities may not see such extreme pressures, the progress that has been made since the mid-1990s in countering social segregation and building mixed communities is likely to stall, if not go into reverse. It is impossible to avoid the conclusion that a fundamental rethink and change of direction will be essential in the near future if the dire consequences of current government policies are to be avoided.

If that rethink is to happen, it will require a renaissance in the planning process. Whereas the early pioneers of planned development, such as Ebenezer Howard, who set out a model for New Garden cities,[13] and ministers such as Lewis Silkin, who put in place the post-war 1947 Town and Country Planning Act, were clear that what was required was visionary planning for a better future, the planning system has evolved over the seven decades since the 1947 Act into something very different, focused narrowly on development control. A disproportionate amount of time and energy goes into determining whether or not individual planning applications should be approved, rather than into generating and building support for comprehensive plans for meeting the future needs of each area in the country. In the current climate it is not surprising that nimbyism continues to flourish. The main issues raised for public debate tend to be whether or not particular proposals for new housing schemes, new commercial developments or new roads should be approved. Even when local authorities try to engage their residents in the process of developing their local plan, which should encapsulate the full range of local needs such as housing, schools, workplaces, transport networks, open space and leisure facilities, and how these are best provided, the debate is all too often hijacked by one or more vocal lobby groups opposed to one particular type of development.

Rebuilding confidence in our capacity to plan, so that we do generate ambitious and imaginative visions for the future, will not come from central government. Central government has a role to play, not least in making clear the scale of provision that is likely to be required to meet the country's future economic, social and environmental needs. It also has a key role to play in identifying areas where strategic growth is necessary in the national interest and in promoting appropriate partnerships or development agencies to make this happen. There also must be a mechanism to ensure that nationally determined needs are cascaded down to each locality, so that the sum of the parts does add up to the required national total. The absence of any such mechanism in the current planning system is its most egregious failing. But the detailed local plans have to be created at a regional and local level if they are to command public confidence. This will call for further devolution of powers (covered in Chapters Six and Seven) and the development of a new generation of enlightened and far-seeing local planners interested in place making – shaping the future of their areas rather than simply reacting to the short-term pressures of development applications. In turn, that will call for brave political leadership at national, regional and local levels. Nationally there has to be recognition of the importance of further devolution of powers within England, within a framework that does ensure that national requirements are met. At a sub-national level there has to be ambition to create better, more prosperous and fairer communities and the courage to back what is necessary against short-term or sectional interests and against the easy option of taking the line of least resistance.

FIVE

Will it fly?

So far I have concentrated on a series of major policy issues, most requiring primary legislation, that have tended to attract high levels of political attention, and often controversy. But the process of government is also full of detail, much of which, while important and significantly impacting on people's lives, rarely attracts media coverage unless things go wrong. In this chapter I cover a number of such issues, the first two relating to Building Regulations. The Building Regulations are designed to protect the safety of those involved in the construction and occupation of buildings. They are there to ensure that what is built is structurally sound, wind- and waterproof, and that it meets the various standards for lighting, ventilation, sound and thermal insulation, energy efficiency and so on necessary to meet the expectations of society, as approved by Parliament, at any given point in time. Almost by definition there is a continuing process of adapting and upgrading the standards both to reflect advances in technology and building techniques and to respond to other pressures, such as the obligation to achieve reductions in carbon emissions. There are also some fine judgements to be made on the best way to promote innovation that will lead to higher standards without adding unreasonable cost.

As in so many other areas of public policy, the Building Regulations prompt very different reactions and points of view. Developers and house-builders generally seek to minimise the imposition of what they often describe as unnecessary additional regulatory burdens, although in some circumstances they recognise that Building Regulations can create a 'level playing field' that allows necessary improvements, for example in energy efficiency standards, to be achieved across the industry, without the most progressive companies being undercut by those that fail to meet proper standards. Conversely, lobbying groups, including those representing environmental interests or the concerns of people with disabilities, generally press for enhancements in the required standards to meet their campaigning objectives. While this reflects a familiar pattern of political debate, the way in which the issues are dealt with in government is in some respects very different. Civil servants in the teams dealing with Building Regulations tend to stay much longer in post than those in other policy divisions, where a three-year turnover pattern is common. They also work with standing committees of experts (in this case BRAC, the Building Regulations Advisory Committee) who do much of the technical work on defining the specific regulatory requirements.

This all tends to foster an assumption that the process by which the Building Regulations are introduced, upgraded or revised is a largely technical one that is not as susceptible to political influence as other policy matters. Yet the impact of Building Regulations can have a profound effect on the way people live their lives. In my period as Minister for Construction, between 1997 and 2001, I held responsibility for the Building Regulations. The three most significant changes to the Building Regulations that I oversaw were the introduction of Part M, which is designed to ensure easy access to housing, particularly for people with mobility impairment, the upgrade of Part B, which deals with fire prevention and safety, and the beginning of a sustained programme to upgrade Part L, the section that deals with energy efficiency. All three had very far-reaching implications and two of the three (Part M and Part L) provoked major political rows. Both followed similar trajectories, from initial industry objection to the raising of standards, through a period of negotiation and discussion, to agreement on a practical way forward that the industry comes to accept. But this benign progression is not always achieved. The dangers inherent in the process are obvious:

1. government being unnerved by industry objections, or unduly influenced by exaggerated threats of adverse consequences or cost increases;

2. conversely, government not paying sufficient heed to industry warnings about potential downsides, or imposing unreasonable extra costs;
3. opportunities for technological advance that will bring real benefits to the public being delayed or compromised by the process of negotiating changes to the Regulations;
4. the public having few opportunities to influence or participate in the discussions because of the highly technical nature of the process.

In this chapter I will focus on the changes to Parts M and L. Fire safety issues are covered more widely in Chapter Nine.

The passage of the Disability Discrimination Act in 1995 reflected real concerns about the extent to which people with disabilities were effectively excluded from large numbers of buildings and services simply because access arrangements were impossible to negotiate, for example in a wheelchair. As well as prompting a range of organisations in both the public and private sectors to review and improve their existing premises, it also naturally led to calls for changes to the Building Regulations to ensure that new homes would from the outset be easily accessible to all. This in effect was seeking to remedy an anomaly, in that Part M of the Building Regulations already required new buildings other than homes to be built in such a way as to allow easy access for those with mobility impairments. There was no particular logic in treating homes any differently from other buildings, while the costs of retrofitting existing homes to make them accessible to disabled people were substantially greater than for making provision in the first place. So, the case for making a change to extend Part M to homes was a strong one.

In response, the Conservative government led by John Major issued a White Paper including a pledge to consult on measures to extend Part M of the Building Regulations to dwellings.[1] This in turn led to the formulation of a set of standards by officials in the then Department of the Environment, working with BRAC, to ensure that new dwellings were constructed with level access and space standards sufficient to allow those with impaired mobility to be able to negotiate the ground floor of the building without difficulty. The standards did not go as far as those promoted by the Joseph Rowntree Foundation, among others, for 'Lifetime Homes', which were designed to allow easy conversion of homes to accommodate wheelchair users, including hoists and lifts, and which therefore had significant additional cost implications and were generally adopted only by specialist housing providers for the elderly and people with disabilities. Nevertheless the proposed access standards set out in a draft Part M of the Building Regulations were welcomed by most disability campaigners as a significant step forward in making homes more easily accessible to people with impaired mobility.

The reaction from house-builders was, however, very different. A whole series of objections were raised, including the practical issues of achieving level access on steeply sloping sites, the risk of water penetration where a doorstep was not provided and the cost of complying with the obligation to provide access to a WC at the dwelling's entry level. It was even argued that people buying new homes should not be expected to pay more so that their home was accessible to people with disabilities. As later developments were to demonstrate, most of the issues could be resolved sensibly and cost-effectively with a little bit of thought and goodwill. Indeed the extra costs trumpeted by the house-builders turned out on detailed examination to be very modest, not least in the context of house price inflation over subsequent years. But, rather than seeking to achieve a negotiated outcome, the then government parked the issue in the 'too difficult' tray. As opposition housing spokesman I was frankly surprised at this 'cave-in' in face of the house-builders' intransigence. It certainly reflected the considerable influence of this industry as a lobbying force, and also the growing power of the advocates of deregulation within the Conservative Party. But in consequence it left the government looking weak and ineffective, and also damaged its reputation among many people with disabilities. It also perpetuated an unsatisfactory situation in which new homes were being built in a way that would pose a serious if not insurmountable obstacle to their ever being occupied or even visited by someone with disabilities. Whatever the reason for their indecision, no progress was made over the following two years and the issue remained unresolved in the run-up to the 1997 general election.

Rather than wait till after the election, I decided early in 1997 to break the log-jam by inviting the Housebuilders Federation and the Joseph Rowntree Foundation to get together to explore the scope for agreement on a way forward that would lead to the extension of Part M to dwellings. Probably because they could see that a Labour victory was likely in the forthcoming election and that, unlike the Conservative government, we would insist on progressing this reform, the house-builders proved more amenable to discussion than they had been when the DoE consultation had been launched two years before. In all events the two parties did meet, and within a relatively short period of time agreement had been reached on most of the issues. It helped that Richard (now Lord) Best, director of the Joseph Rowntree Foundation, was able to call on the experience of a number of housing associations that, like the Rowntree Trust in York, were already building to accessibility standards. This enabled them to demonstrate on the basis of practical experience that ramped rather than stepped access was feasible on most sites and that there was no greater risk of water penetration with level access, provided that the doorways were properly designed. The additional costs associated with most of the necessary adaptations, including wider doors and more accessible locations for switches, were minimal and even the entry-level WC proved a less serious cost obstacle than had initially been feared. An exemption allowing stepped access in exceptional circumstances where it was simply impossible to provide level or ramped access also helped to dispel industry objections. So, literally within a few months of coming into government in May 1997, we were able to announce our intention to extend Part M to dwellings, with the house-builders now only seeking to postpone the introduction of the new regulations rather than opposing them outright. Following the preparation of the necessary Regulatory Impact Assessment, which demonstrated the extensive benefits of the proposed changes and the modest costs involved, we laid the Regulations giving effect to the changes before Parliament in October 1998, and they came into force in October 1999.

The only obstacle to implementation now was a quixotic press campaign to 'Save the Great British doorstep'! This was quickly dealt with through a very helpful tip-off from one of our department's press officers that within a stone's throw of our central London office was a fine terrace of Georgian housing with level access. If the Great British doorstep was not a requirement for our finest domestic architectural heritage, we could hardly deny Barratts or Berkeley Homes the opportunity to follow suit. Indeed one of the interesting outcomes of this saga was the absence of any significant complaints from the house-builders once the new regulations had come into force. They simply got on with building to the new standards with scarcely a whimper. The lesson from this saga is a simple one that governments need to be firm when confronted with unconvincing, albeit vociferous, campaigns from whatever source.

The change to Part M was a relatively simple process by comparison with Part L. It was a one-off change that required little new design or technological input. By contrast, upgrading the energy efficiency of housing and buildings more widely would prove a much more complex challenge. I have already (Chapter Four) referred to the legacy of poorly insulated and energy-inefficient housing built in the housing boom years following the Second World War. The older pre-war housing stock was equally problematic, but that essentially reflected the prevailing attitudes of a time in which fuel was plentiful and relatively cheap and there was no obvious imperative to improve the energy performance of buildings. The perpetuation of those attitudes through until the 1970s left a huge backlog of supposedly modern homes that made profligate use of energy and proved difficult and expensive to keep warm in winter once fuel prices began to rise significantly. But while the country became increasingly addicted to home improvements, the public's clear preference was for visible and cosmetic changes – new kitchens and bathrooms and perhaps the addition of a conservatory – rather than for measures to improve their property's energy performance. In fact many of those cosmetic improvements actually worsened the property's energy efficiency, but because they generally added value while invisible energy improvements didn't, there was no market pressure to prompt either homeowners or house-builders to raise energy-performance standards.

In this situation action by government was essential if things were to change. The weapons available were the usual carrots and sticks. Grants, for example to encourage loft insulation, worked, but they were less successful as a stimulus to new technological advances, such as the introduction of condensing boilers. Targeted public sector intervention to tackle fuel poverty through projects such as Neighbourhood Energy Action also worked to a degree, but essentially were about applying sticking plasters to the wound, as for example through draught-sealing around doors and windows and secondary glazing. Having myself helped to promote a number of such initiatives in the 1980s, it was depressing now to see how often they were required even in relatively new homes that had been built in the preceding two decades. The clear message was that applying palliatives was not enough. A lasting solution depended on raising the standards required by Building Regulations. While the Major government did conduct a review of Part L of the Building Regulations in 1994, in contrast to its decision to duck the review of Part M, this still left a long way to go if new homes in Britain were to match the much higher energy-performance standards being achieved in many other European countries. And, as with Part M, the house-builders were implacably opposed to any new regulatory obligation to raise standards.

This was the position we inherited in 1997. We also faced the imminent Kyoto conference on climate change, and with John Prescott leading the British delegation to that conference this provided a helpful impetus for his department to undertake a further review of Part L, despite the protestations of the house-builders. The terms of the review launched in early 1998 made this very clear:

> The aim of this review is to establish the maximum possible contribution that can be made to the CO2 targets through the Building Regulations whilst observing proportionality, allowing flexibility for designers and avoiding unreasonable technical risks or excessive cost.[2]

The conclusion that emerged from addressing this question was that instead of a one-off uplift in the requirements we needed to set out a route-map with a series of uplifts, phased in a way that took account of the industry's capacity to innovate, that would over a period of time allow the ratcheting up of standards without having to risk unreasonable technical leaps of faith or cost hikes along the way. By phasing the programme with a series of milestones, we could give certainty to the industry, whose supply chain could gear up to deliver the materials and technology necessary to meet the progressively higher standards in a cost-effective way. This approach was ultimately to lead to the commitment, made some years later when Yvette Cooper was minister, to the 2016 Zero Carbon target, accompanied by the Code for Sustainable Homes, which defined the levels of performance that needed to be reached at the various milestones along the route.[3] It also generated the Zero Carbon Hub, an industry–government partnership to help identify the most appropriate and cost-effective technical solutions to the progressively higher demands that the Code and the route-map imposed.[4] This approach effectively addressed the first three of the four challenges identified earlier. It made clear government's determination to achieve transformational change. It did so in a way that responded to the industry's legitimate concerns, and it provided a framework in which there was a real incentive for innovation and technical advances. Perhaps the most interesting example of this was the 'Aim C 4' initiative involving the Zero Carbon Hub and house-builders such as Barratts, Crest Nicholson and Stewart Milne, who set themselves the challenge of exploring how they might deliver Code Level 4 standards of energy efficiency without increasing costs above those required to meet Code Level 3 requirements.[5] Securing industry buy-in to the ambitious carbon-reduction agenda was a major step forward. Even if the ultimate goal of Zero Carbon was not reached (it was abandoned by the Conservative government) the energy performance of new buildings, and particularly of new homes, improved out of all recognition in the first decade and a half of the 21st century. Of course this is only one step in the right direction. The massive task of retrofitting the great majority of existing homes that remain substandard in energy-efficiency terms is still outstanding, but at least we are no longer perpetuating it through the continued production of poorly insulated and poorly performing new ones.

The one area in which progress has been less obvious is the public's awareness of the issue and its involvement in the process of improving energy performance in housing. Such research as has been conducted[6] suggests that there has been some advance in public awareness about energy performance in housing, but it remains an 'also-ran' in terms of the priority afforded to it in comparison with other factors influencing decisions on buying or renovating a home. This helps to explain the abject failure of the Coalition government's Green Deal plan to stimulate investment in improving the energy efficiency of existing homes. The Green Deal was a classic illustration of a basically good idea made unworkable by over-complex engineering. The procedures for assessing the appropriate energy-efficiency measures to be adopted, and the arrangements for the loan to finance the works and subsequent charge on the property, were complex and difficult for the public to understand. They and other scheme rules designed to protect the public from cowboy builders added layers of bureaucracy and cost, undermining any hope that the Green Deal might attract the public's imagination and support. While the issue of raising the energy performance of the country's housing stock continues to be seen as a relatively low priority for the public, policy developments will remain dependent on government initiatives, as described in this chapter, and will be a technically driven rather than consumer-led process.

Another supposedly 'technical' issue with which I was involved between 1997 and 2001 was a measure designed to streamline the house-buying and selling process, which later became highly controversial. The history of the 'sellers' pack' is instructive and illustrates how policy initiatives that initially appear sound, and indeed have been carefully prepared and piloted with the active participation of key stakeholders, can easily unravel over a period of time, particularly if they become a focus for political controversy. The origin of the 'sellers' pack' proposal came from a 1997 Labour manifesto commitment to make the house-buying and selling process easier and less prone to delay, frustration and abortive costs. As the housing market had recovered through the

1990s from the 1989 recession, so problems such as 'gazumping' (where prospective buyers whose offer for a property has been accepted find that the seller has subsequently accepted a higher offer from another party) began to reappear. Although the newly elected Labour government was not short of suggestions from a range of different sources of 'quick fix' remedies for the problem, its response was not to rush to conclusions but, rather, to commission research on how the house-buying and selling process was working, with recommendations for improvements. The conclusion of this review was unequivocal:

> The housing transaction process does not seem to be designed with the interests of the consumer in mind ... there is a general dissatisfaction with the process as a whole.[7]

The principal weakness in the process was identified as the long period of time generally taken to move from the point where an offer is accepted to the exchange of contracts. During this period, typically lasting around two months, there is much scope for things to go wrong, subsequent research suggesting that one prospective sale in five fails during this period. For example, unforeseen problems in the condition of the property may emerge from a survey, or closer examination of the terms of a lease may throw up unwelcome restrictions. Additionally, in a rising market there is always the risk of 'gazumping'. One means of tackling this would have been to follow the Scottish model where a binding contract is created once an offer is accepted. However, the research team concluded that this would not guarantee to stop gazumping, and would have significant disadvantages, including a risk of an increased number of failed bids and abortive costs. So, rather than seeking to make the contract binding at the point when the offer is accepted, the team recommended practical measures to speed up the process and remove or greatly reduce the scope for things to go wrong. By having most of the key documentation – including title deeds, leases, planning consents and conditions, covenants, warranties and guarantees, a draft contract and a survey – available at the start of the process, in the form of a Home Information Pack

(HIP) or 'seller's pack' as it was often described, the transaction process after acceptance of an offer would be very much quicker, with less likelihood of unexpected 'show-stoppers' emerging, for example from a survey. It would also save abortive legal and survey costs.

At the same time other related reforms were encouraged, such as a move towards electronic conveyancing, greater use of automated valuations, encouraging buyers to get 'in principle' mortgage finance agreement in advance and improved bridging loan products to help break chain log-jams, to save time and cost to the public. The proposed package of measures was comprehensive and thorough, and received a generally warm welcome from most informed commentators. Only two issues emerged as potential difficulties. First was the degree to which a buyer could rely on the survey, which would have been commissioned by the seller. Here the answer was obviously to make the surveyor liable to the buyer as well as to the seller. Second, there were worries in low-value, low-demand areas of the country that the initial up-front cost to the seller of commissioning the HIP would be disproportionate. The advice that I received from many professionals involved in home-buying and selling was that a market would rapidly develop with strong competition between potential HIP providers and this would keep the cost down. In any event, it was expected that most estate agents would not require up-front payment from potential sellers for the HIP, but would recover the cost from the sale proceeds. There might be a need for additional special provision in very low-value areas, but this was certainly not a 'show-stopper'. In any case the overall economic effects of the introduction of HIPs were expected to be positive, with a significant reduction in abortive costs. The shift in the balance of risk from buyer to seller was clearly helpful to first-time buyers, and as most sellers were also looking to buy a replacement home, they would gain on the swings what they stood to lose on the roundabout.

Following a largely positive response to the consultation that the government undertook, it was agreed that the scheme should be piloted to allow for the practicalities to be tested and for a further assessment to be made on the potential impact of the scheme before giving it the go-ahead. Given this prudent approach, one might have expected a smooth and easy implementation. The reality was very different. Although the pilot in Bristol was concluded successfully, and the necessary legislation introduced, the Homes Bill did not complete its parliamentary passage in the short 2000–01 session leading up to the general election. As I was moved from the Housing and Planning brief to Local and Regional Government following the general election, I had no direct involvement in the later stages of this saga, but watched with increasing alarm as a sensible reforming measure that would have brought considerable benefits to home-buyers (particularly first-time buyers) was allowed to crash.

Why did this happen? In my view there were four principal reasons

1. *Loss of momentum.* Following the 2001 general election, the necessary legislation to give effect to the plan, making it a legal obligation to have a HIP available when a property was put on the market, was not immediately reintroduced. Charlie Falconer, who took over the Housing and Planning brief, was supportive of the HIP proposal and does not believe that there was any political reluctance to legislate. In his view the most likely cause of delay was pressure on the legislative timetable because of the large number of Bills in the queue for this first post-election session of Parliament. But the absence of the HIP provisions from the legislative programme was still surprising. They had been part of a Bill that was before Parliament in the previous session. The other measures in that Bill, covering the prevention and relief of homelessness, were brought straight back in a new Bill in 2001. Nor was there any clear reason for giving priority to the homelessness provisions as opposed to HIPs, as both were manifesto commitments. In all events, the non-appearance of legislation giving effect to the policy was seen as an indication that the government was less committed than it had been to this reform, and it certainly gave comfort to some groups, mainly estate agents, who were opposed to it. Momentum is an important factor in politics. Governments with a clear agenda and commitment to implement their policies tend, unless the policies are seriously flawed, to get their way – certainly when they have a parliamentary majority

of more than 160, as the re-elected Labour government had in 2001. By contrast, governments that appear to be less than whole-heartedly committed to particular measures (see Chapter Seven) or that prevaricate over their introduction often end up with egg on their face.

2. *Changing ministerial responsibility.* The problem was compounded by frequent changes of minister. The process that led to the HIP proposal was initiated when Hilary Armstrong was Housing Minister between 1997 and 1999. As I had worked closely with her, the transfer of responsibility to me in 1999 did not lead to any loss of momentum, but frequent subsequent changes did not help. Charlie Falconer was Housing and Planning Minister for just one year (2001–02) before his promotion to the post of Lord Chancellor. His successor, Jeff Rooker, also held the post for one year only. In 2003, Keith Hill took over and injected a new sense of urgency. On his watch the legislation was revived and passed into law, with June 2007 set as the date for the scheme to go live.[8] However, the 2005 general election that came first led to another change of minister, with Yvette Cooper taking over. Her chief interest in the measure was as a vehicle to promote Energy Performance Certificates, as part of her push for low-carbon homes, and when the by now emboldened opponents of HIPs launched a sustained attack on the policy she agreed to drop the requirement for a survey, in the hope that this would defuse opposition by reducing the cost of producing a HIP. The policy was refocused towards the promotion of lower-carbon homes, which, while a worthwhile aim, was not the main purpose of the exercise. Indeed without a survey in the HIP, its likely effectiveness as a means of speeding up transactions was severely compromised and several of the former supporters of the scheme, particularly from the consumer perspective, withdrew their backing. Further ministerial changes followed with Caroline Flint's appointment as Housing Minister in 2007, she in turn being succeeded by Margaret Beckett in 2008 and John Healey in 2009. But by now the original purpose of the policy had been largely forgotten and the filleted remains were left on an

unedifying downward trajectory to what became an inevitable cancellation by the incoming Coalition government in 2010.

3. *Failure to sell the idea to the public.* Perhaps because the project was founded on technical assessments by professionals and because, at least in its first years, it enjoyed strong support from consumer representatives, the government did not give sufficient attention to building public support by explaining the advantages to the large numbers of potential beneficiaries. First-time buyers, in particular, stood to gain substantially from the introduction of sellers' packs, yet, at a time when rising home prices were beginning to pose a serious challenge to many prospective buyers very little was done to promote the project as a means of improving their prospects of successfully completing the purchase of a suitable home. At a time when most buyers depended on their mortgage lender's valuation and did not themselves commission a survey, the requirement for a survey in the seller's pack was a real benefit without any cost. For those buyers who did commission a survey, the risk of abortive costs if the transaction failed was also removed. Yet few if any of the potential beneficiaries were aware of this. Nor was the case for speeding up transactions in order to reduce the risk of gazumping promoted effectively. So, when, in the later stages, opposition from professional interests began to mount, there was no strong public and consumer lobby to come to its defence.

4. *Emboldened opposition.* This political vacuum was inevitably filled, not by impartial analysts, but by emboldened opponents who focused remorselessly on what they saw as the weaknesses of the scheme. The first of these was the potential cost to the seller, to which as we have already seen there were real answers, both in the development of a market to provide HIPs and in the efficiency savings and removal of abortive costs. A well-informed public would, in my judgement have backed the scheme, but in the absence of this voice, critics, among whom estate agents were dominant, were able to spread alarm. The real concern among estate agents was that the requirement to prepare a 'seller's pack' before putting a property on the market would deter some potential sellers who might not have seriously intended selling their home, but were pleased

to see it on the market so as to get a feel for its potential value. The rapid development of automated valuations of course provided quick and cheap alternative means to get this information, but this was no comfort to estate agents who wanted to maximise the number of properties in their 'shop window'. Had the scheme been introduced earlier, while the housing market was still buoyant, these self-interested concerns could more easily have been dealt with, but in the troubled conditions post 2007, with prices tumbling in many areas and few people putting properties on the market, the scare stories about HIPs damaging an already weak market gained traction. As often happens when a political initiative is seen as trouble, the media close in for a 'kill'. Wilder and wilder claims about the potential costs and negative impact of the scheme were aired, but were never effectively rebutted. But, as I have already shown, by this stage the scheme had been so compromised that it was difficult even for its supporters to make a convincing case for its survival.

While some government initiatives, such as extension of the Building Regulations and the proposed reform of the home-buying and selling process, are the product of a well-defined policy-development process,[9] others are thrust onto the agenda by events. How government responds will often determine whether or not the issue becomes a cause célèbre or recedes into obscurity. The next two case studies were both the product of events, and neither has received much publicity other than in the areas immediately affected. However, if the outcomes had been less successful I suspect that both could have prompted major national media condemnation.

The City of Bath was largely built of the eponymous stone quarried and mined from local sites. The largest and most significant of these was Combe Down, a village located just a mile or so south of the city. Between the 1730s and 1840s a huge quantity of stone was extracted, much of it by mining underneath land that was progressively developed in the 19th and 20th centuries for housing. Although the scale of mining declined in the later 19th century, some extraction continued into the 20th century. As the seams were worked out, the mining increasingly compromised the stability of the area. By the late 1980s there was growing local concern about the risk of a collapse. A survey undertaken in the early 1990s revealed, in the words of the excellent local history,[10] that:

> a large number of mine roof collapses had occurred since the mine had closed and the majority of the original timber support had rotted away.
>
> The highly fractured roof had been allowed to sag, increasing the risk of further roof falls. A number of pillars had become overstressed due to the high extraction ratio and were effectively providing minimal support to the roof. It was seen as only a matter of time before significant pillar failure occurred leading to widespread surface subsidence.

Despite the obvious risk, applications made by Bath City Council to the then DoE for financial assistance towards the cost of remediation work were unsuccessful. The only fund available to support the costs of such work, Derelict Land Grant, had been exhausted in the time of the Major government and there appeared to be no obvious means of financing the costs of stabilising the site. This was the position when, in 1998, Don Foster, the engaging and effective MP for Bath, sought a meeting with me to discuss the issue. After setting out the nature of the problem and the risk to his constituents, he invited me to visit Combe Down to see for myself the condition of the mine. I had no hesitation in accepting this offer, despite the clear reservations of officials in the department, who had no doubt written the refusal letters in response to Bath's previous requests for help. The visit was, as Don Foster had probably anticipated, a real eye-opener. There was no question as to the scale of the problem – huge, cavernous areas with a roof haphazardly supported by often frighteningly thin and seriously eroded stone columns. Perhaps most shocking to me was to be able to hear, quite clearly, conversations going on above ground level, so close was the mine to the surface. This powerfully reinforced the case for action to safeguard a community comprising some 700 homes and around 1,400 people living under a constant threat of disaster.

I left Combe Down with absolutely no doubt that we had to respond positively and assist Bath and North East Somerset Council (as it had become from 1996) to take remedial action to stabilise Combe Down. There were two obstacles to be overcome. First was the absence of any mechanism to fund the works, following the demise of the former Derelict Land Grant programme. Second was the need to secure political agreement for what would inevitably involve significant public expenditure. On both points I was fortunate to secure the full support of John Prescott, who recognised the parallel between the situation in Combe Down and that in many coal-mining communities, vulnerable to subsidence and unexpected ground collapses. So, English Partnerships were given the task of developing a new Land Stabilisation Programme to support remedial works in areas, like Combe Down, left with serious inherited problems from their mining past. I doubt whether this would have happened without ministerial intervention. By mid-1999 the new programme was operational and Bath and North East Somerset Council had secured funding for a full appraisal of the works needed to stabilise the site. Given the scale of the area affected, and the potential environmental impacts of various stabilisation options, the process was neither quick nor easy. Initial thinking in the mid-1990s that pulverised fuel ash could be used as a filler had been abandoned because of a risk of contaminants leaking into the aquifer. Instead the decision was taken to use foamed concrete, some 590,000 cubic metres of which were required, making it at the time the largest application of foamed concrete anywhere in the world. But with sustained government support, including subsequent approval from my colleague Keith Hill for total expenditure in excess of £150 million, the works were successfully completed in 2009 and the villagers of Combe Down could breathe easily again. The story could, however, have very easily had a different outcome.

So too could one of the other early challenges I faced in government in 1998. Initially I was unsure why the issue landed on my desk. Technically, it did fall within my Construction, Building Regulations, and Planning responsibilities, but did it really require intensive ministerial involvement? I rapidly concluded that it was seen as a high-risk topic on which both

officials and my more senior ministerial colleagues were happy
to avoid being seen as the person responsible if things went
wrong. So I found myself in the summer of 1998 overseeing the
eradication of termites in the North Devon village of Saunton.
How did the problem arise? While they have traditionally
been a serious threat to timber buildings in many tropical and
sub-tropical parts of the world, causing in the judgement of
the Building Research Establishment (BRE) 'more damage to
buildings worldwide than all other pests of buildings combined',
termites had been largely unknown in Britain, because of the
climate. According to the BRE:

> the Saunton termites are believed to have arrived as
> a small number of workers and reproductive insects
> in packing materials around a plant imported from
> Southern Europe more than 10 years ago. They then
> appear to have become established in the soil in a
> greenhouse and managed to survive and expand their
> distribution despite the colder climate in the UK.[11]

Their presence and potentially damaging impact was first
detected in 1994, when

> judgement at the time was that localised fluid
> treatments would be an appropriate response
> commensurate with the low level of activity observed
> and low risk expected so far north of the previously
> known limits of distribution of this pest species.[12]

However, the measures taken by a local contractor at that time
clearly failed to eliminate the termites, whose presence was once
again confirmed in spring 1998. The inspection that followed
revealed a much more worrying picture:

> Evidence of serious damage and of very large
> numbers of active termites confirmed a major
> infestation representing a completely new situation,
> requiring a radically new approach to its eradication.[13]

At least one neighbouring property had also been infested, and evidence of termite activity was found over a wide area. More worrying still was the advice I received that in certain circumstances the species of termite at Saunton (Reticulitermes lucifugus) could develop wings and fly in a swarm. If this were to happen it would become very difficult if not impossible to contain the threat of much more widespread infestation. To add to the worry I was advised that:

> In regions where termites are indigenous the concept of total eradication from the natural environment is not a viable option.[14]

We were therefore in a race against time to find a means to eradicate the Saunton termites before they spread underground or by winged flight to the point where containment was no longer possible. Their survival over the previous decade in the temperate climate and sandy soil of North Devon was a clear indication that our traditional dependence on the British climate to protect us from this pest was no longer to be taken for granted.

Advised by an international academic expert on termites from Imperial College, the BRE developed an eradication programme using a substance, Hexaflumuron, which, once ingested, would effectively sterilise the insects. This was to be incorporated in baits, large numbers of which would be installed in the core area of termite activity, which had a 75-metre radius. Surrounding this treatment zone there would be a wider intensive monitoring zone with a 200-metre radius and a continuous perimeter 'fence' filled with devices designed to detect any evidence of a spread of termite activity. Beyond this would be a third, yet more extensive buffer zone with a 500-metre radius to prevent activity, such as the movement of materials that could unintentionally allow the spread of previously undetected termites. The scale and extent of this installation gives a very clear indication of the seriousness with which the threat was treated and the care taken to prevent any further spread. However, the plan depended on the Saunton termites responding as expected to the baits that were installed in autumn 1998. In the event, the monitoring revealed relatively quickly that the termites were not taking the bait. While other species of termite (R. santoniensis, kept, hopefully for research purposes only, at the BRE) had in earlier tests responded as hoped, it appeared that the Saunton variety (R. lucifugus) was repelled by the Hexaflumuron and further tests were required to see if this effect could be countered. Fortunately there was a window of opportunity over the winter while the termites were dormant, but it was essential to have an answer in place by early spring, when termite activity could again be anticipated. After various further tests it was found that the addition of fungal extracts to the bait would mask the repellent characteristics of Hexaflumuron and a new series of baits were prepared to be put in place as soon as the termites were seen to be active again. In early spring 1999 the new baits were installed and this time they worked as planned. Within a very short period there was clear evidence of their impact:

> The first evidence of significant field consumption of hexaflumuron was detected in March 1999. During the scheduled visits in April and May no further expansion of the area of activity was noted.... By July no termite activity of any form could be detected in any of the soil-based monitoring devices or baits ...[15]

This wasn't quite the end of the story, for we had been warned that some isolated groups of termites might survive the eradication of the main colony and there was therefore a risk of recurrence. So, continued monitoring took place for more than a year. The last ground-based termite activity was detected in April 2000, after which there was a welcome absence of any sign of termite life in Saunton. The threat of further spread had not materialised and, unlike the earlier attempt to eliminate the pests, this one had achieved its goal. For the moment at least, Britain has managed to protect its shores from termite infestation.

What broader lessons can be drawn from this incident? First is the interesting and recurring issue of the border between central and local government responsibilities. On the surface it might appear odd that central government was involved at all. This was a local incident in just one part of the country. However, had the Saunton termites survived and spread, the potential consequences for many other areas were dire. Indeed the failure of the first local attempt to tackle the problem effectively reinforces the case for national government involvement. As with the Combe Down episode, the specialist and complex nature of the challenge would have strained the resources of most district councils. At the time, the department was very much at the heart of government's relationship with the construction industry and so had both the expertise and contacts necessary to handle the challenges posed by the discovery of the Saunton termites. The BRE, although privatised, was still closely related to the Department for the Environment, Transport and the Regions (DETR), which was well placed to call in all the necessary resources to ensure a successful outcome. Following the 2001 general election this changed, with a transfer of the former construction-sponsorship role to what is now the Department for Business, Innovation & Skills, and a winding down of many of the research and promotional activities previously undertaken by DETR for the industry. I am not sure that, were the termite infestation to recur today, central government would be as well placed as it proved to be in 1998 to deliver a properly coordinated response.

A second reflection prompted by the Combe Down and Saunton experiences is the importance of ministers' excluding party political considerations from decision making in such incidents. Both occurred in areas of the country where the Labour Party had little realistic prospect of winning either control of the local council or the parliamentary constituency. A crude analysis of the party political implications in both instances would suggest that there was little advantage to be gained by the Labour Party from government intervention and, in the case of Combe Down, very substantial investment of public funds. Had such considerations been allowed to influence decision making there could have been a very different outcome. In the climate of public opinion where politicians are often depicted as being primarily motivated by personal or party political interests rather than the public interest, it is important to recognise the extent to which significant decisions are and should be taken altruistically and with priority rightly being accorded to the overriding public interest. I well recall a brief conversation with the Conservative peer Lord Banham in the course of a visit to

Cornwall when he went out of his way to thank me for helping to ensure that Cornwall continued to benefit from European Union funding in the late 1990s and early 2000s even though, as he acknowledged, there was no party political benefit likely to accrue to the Labour Party from this (the county was then, with the sole exception of the Falmouth and Camborne seat, largely dominated by Liberal Democrats and Conservatives). Doing the right thing, irrespective of short-term party political advantage, is the hallmark of a confident and mature democracy. That is why it is important to acknowledge and publicise such incidents so as to counter the prevailing mood of cynicism about the motivation of those engaged in the political process.

SIX

A mayor for London

By almost any criteria the 20th century proved to be the high-water mark of centralism in England. A series of disparate but very powerful influences all pushed policy in a centralising direction for almost the entire 100 years. The war-time imperative of maximising military and industrial output led to unprecedented national controls being introduced across a huge swathe of activities in the 1910s and 1940s. The Fabian quest for a more egalitarian society, coupled with the confidence of the political Left in the benign role of the state in advancing economic efficiency and social justice, gave added impetus to the centralising instinct, particularly in the immediate aftermath of the Second World War. So too, despite her party's proclaimed support for the 'shrinking of the state' did Margaret Thatcher's dislike of political opposition from local government and trade unions. The media too contributed as national newspapers and new broadcast media increasingly came to dominate the channels of communication and as they highlighted the problems of 'post code lotteries' whereby individuals lost out through local standards falling below national norms.

Only at the two book ends of the century, in the years before the First World War when Irish Home Rule was on the agenda, and in the late 1990s when devolution to Scotland, Wales, Northern Ireland and London became key government objectives, was the remorseless one-way centralising tendency challenged, and even in these years other factors continued to push in a centralist direction.

The outcome has been an unprecedented shift in the balance of power between the central and the local. Whereas the evolution of the British economy and governance in the 18th and 19th centuries was to a substantial degree promoted locally, whether by industrialists or by civic leaders firmly rooted in the rapidly expanding cities in the Midlands, northern England and Scotland, by the end of the 20th century the levers of power were overwhelmingly held in London and Westminster. Even within London power had been centralised, with the former Greater London Council (GLC) being abolished in 1986 and the powers of the 32 London boroughs being severely curtailed by central government. Key decisions affecting London's infrastructure and public services were almost all taken or determined by central government and its agencies. The very existence of a Government Office for London and the post of Minister for London spoke volumes about the extent of central control.

When Tony Blair formed his first government in May 1997 I was appointed to the role of Minister for London, but with the brief of restoring a democratic structure for city-wide government in the capital – replacing but not replicating the GLC. This was one strand in the new Labour government's devolution agenda, alongside the devolved structures also being created in Scotland, Wales and Northern Ireland.

Whereas in these other cases a lot of thought had been given, particularly in Scotland, to the question of how the devolved bodies would be structured and precisely what powers should be devolved, the London agenda was to a very large degree a blank sheet of paper. Yes, there was a commitment to the creation of a democratically elected city-wide authority and a presumption that this would be a streamlined strategic body and not a large bureaucracy, which is how the former GLC had, for all its virtues, been widely perceived. But as to the structure of the new authority, how it would be elected, what powers it would have and how these were to be exercised, all this had to be determined. The reason why no work had been done in opposition on these issues was a simple but fundamental difference of opinion between Tony Blair, who wanted a new authority to be led by a directly elected mayor, and the Shadow Secretary of State for the Environment, Frank Dobson, who favoured a more traditional local government structure under which the leader would be elected by the councillors. Directly elected mayors feature prominently in the local governance models of many other countries, but in the UK the role of mayor had evolved over the 19th and 20th centuries into a ceremonial one. Quite why the British model of local governance had not followed a similar pattern to that seen in many American, European and other countries is a fascinating question, but not one for this chapter. The outcome, however, left the elected leaders of most British local authorities a less visible public presence than their counterparts in other countries. In the course of working up the governance model for the new London-wide authority we invited several mayors from other countries to come to London to advise us on their experience. In the course of one such visit I was struck how the mayor of New Orleans was immediately recognised and almost mobbed by a group of youngsters visiting London from that city who spotted 'our Mayor' as he walked with me through Trafalgar Square. It was difficult to imagine any British local government leader attracting similar attention.

Because of the difference of opinion between Tony Blair and Frank Dobson, no detailed planning as to how the new authority might best work was undertaken while we were in opposition, unlike the plans for the Scottish Parliament, which had been the subject of extensive work and consultation. In the early months of 1997 I met with Andrew Turnbull, then permanent secretary at the DoE, to discuss the opposition's main policy proposals in the areas for which I held shadow responsibility – housing, construction and London. Such meetings are just about the only formal contact between the civil service and opposition politicians, even though immediately following a change of government the civil service will be expected to implement the incoming government's whole policy agenda. I have often thought that this lack of engagement between civil servants and opposition politicians is one of the weaknesses of our system of government, resulting in some policies appearing in party manifestos with little thought having been given to the potential implementation difficulties. There was a notable difference in the nature of the discussions between me and Andrew Turnbull on the three subjects. On the first two I had prepared short papers setting out our priorities if we were to form the next government. The discussion focused on the practical steps that the civil service would have to arrange in the early months of the new government in order to give effect to these priorities. When we met to discuss our plans for London I had to explain to Andrew why it had not been possible to prepare a similar paper. Instead we explored some of the issues that would need to be worked through if the incoming Prime Minister (assuming we won the election) wanted to proceed with a mayoral form of governance in London. He clearly understood the need to have a high-calibre team of civil servants available to start work immediately following the general election to take forward the planning of what would be an entirely novel form of city-wide government in Britain.

Tony Blair clearly wanted a new style of government, headed by a directly elected mayor able to give highly visible leadership to London, rather than a more traditional local government structure. Following his election victory in May 1997, Frank Dobson was offered a different post as Secretary of State for Health, leaving the way open for a new mayoral-led structure of government for London. John Prescott, the Deputy Prime Minister, who now headed the relevant department, renamed the DETR, shared some of Frank Dobson's Old Labour instincts but made it clear that the new authority which the government was committed to introduce would be headed by a directly elected mayor, and as Minister for London I was given the task of working up the detailed model. It was a remarkable opportunity that I seized with great enthusiasm, but also a degree of apprehension over the work needed to be completed to an incredibly tight timetable.

As part of the wider devolution agenda, it had been agreed that a referendum should be held to approve (or not) the government's planned new Scottish Parliament and Welsh Assembly, and similarly a referendum would be held in London to secure public endorsement for the new city-wide authority. The Scottish and Welsh referenda were already planned for early autumn in 1997. Without a detailed proposition to put to the London electorate, there was no realistic prospect of meeting the same timetable in London, but with London council elections due in May 1998 there was clearly a good opportunity to hold the referendum on the proposed new London-wide authority on the same day.

To meet that timetable, detailed proposals on the new authority would need to be published in a Green Paper for consultation in late July 1997, to be followed by a White Paper taking account of the consultation responses in early spring 1998. This would be the basis for the proposal to be put to the London electorate.

Work began immediately with a very strong team of civil servants assigned to the task, initially under the leadership of Robin Young, the head of the Government Office for London, and subsequently Genie Turton, who took over when Robin moved on promotion to another department. As a newly appointed minister I took great comfort from the high calibre of the civil service team and their obvious enthusiasm for the task. As officials they had literally a few days earlier been working for a government that had abolished the GLC and refused to acknowledge the democratic deficit this had left. Now they were pulling out all the stops to create a new, democratic structure for London government not based on existing models but requiring innovative and creative responses to the variety of challenges that we identified as the work progressed. From my previous encounters, I knew that at their best senior civil servants were outstandingly capable, and the detailed policy-analysis work undertaken by the team of officials set up to develop the new London authority fully lived up to my expectations.

Within a reasonably short period of time we had identified and worked through the key issues that had to be resolved if we were to establish an effective new authority that could deliver practical and cost-effective outcomes for London. Crucial issues were the powers and responsibilities that would be delegated to the new body, how the mayor would exercise his powers and be held to account, how the new authority would interact with the other related bodies, including the London boroughs, and how it would be financed. Our conclusions were set out for consultation in a Green Paper[1] published coincidentally, but perhaps symbolically, on the 100th day of the new government.

The key messages in the Green Paper were that the new authority would be:

- *democratic* – returning city-wide government to London with an executive mayor, directly elected by the whole electorate of

London and held accountable by an assembly whose function was essentially one of scrutiny;

- *strategic* – focusing on the key issues that had to be addressed across the whole of London, such as transport, and not duplicating the work of the other bodies, including the London boroughs, which would continue to hold responsibility for local service delivery;
- *streamlined* – unlike the former GLC, which had over 100 elected members and a huge bureaucracy, the new authority would be deliberately small and focused;
- *inclusive* – with a strong emphasis on involving the full range of interested parties, including business and the voluntary sector, and sensitive to the needs and aspirations of London's increasingly diverse population;
- *influential* – led by a high-profile mayor speaking up for London both nationally and internationally and able to promote positive outcomes for London beyond the limits of the services specifically devolved to the authority.

This was in many respects a ground-breaking prospectus, very different to the traditional structures of local government and light years away from the former GLC. Directly elected by the people of London, the mayor would have one of the largest mandates in any European country, second only to the president of France, and the opportunity to exercise a powerful influence on the future of our capital city. Yet, despite its novelty and the lack of any UK precedents for a powerful but accountable mayor, the Green Paper's proposals were very positively received in most quarters. A measure of the public's support was the extent to which the structures that we put in place in the summer of 2000 very closely reflected those proposed in the Green Paper.

In the months following the Green Paper's publication detailed work continued on the 'nuts and bolts' of the new authority and some of the broad-brush proposals were refined in response both to the consultation and to further research undertaken through the summer and autumn of 1997 on lessons to be learned from mayoral systems of government in other countries. So, the Supplementary Vote system of election was adopted to ensure that the mayor would have a clear mandate and avoid the risk of a 'lowest common denominator' candidate winning without strong first-preference vote support and owing their election mainly to redistributed second-preference votes. Such an outcome could have arisen if we had adopted other proportional voting systems. Similarly, the decision to opt for relatively large assembly constituencies, generally combining two or three London boroughs, reflected strong advice we had received on the risks of assembly members' support bring 'bought' by the mayor through targeted investment in their areas – a vulnerability in some American mayoral models.

The London boroughs that had initially shown some apprehension about the prospect of a powerful mayor trampling all over their turf were increasingly reassured as we made clear our commitment to an inclusive, consensual and strategic authority. There would be no return to the framework when the GLC had existed, under which some services were the responsibility of both the boroughs and the city-wide authority and there was substantial scope for conflict between the two tiers. Planning was the one area where there was, of necessity, some shared decision making, but we structured arrangements so that the mayor's powers would remain focused on strategic decisions embodied in the London Plan, with the boroughs determining most local decisions. Subsequent changes have tilted the playing field more in the mayor's favour.

At the same time agreement had to be secured from other government departments to the devolution of some of their powers to the mayor. Transport officials were nervous about surrendering some of their control and power to the mayor and Transport for London (TfL), the new functional body that we proposed to create as the delivery agent. However, as transport had, since May 1997, become part of the Deputy Prime Minister's department (DETR), and as John Prescott was fully supportive of the devolution agenda, their scope for resisting a significant package of transport power's being devolved to the mayor and TfL was limited. This was in marked contrast to the position four years later, when the devolution of transport responsibilities to elected regional assemblies in other English regions was under discussion. By then, transport was once again in a separate department, and neither its secretary of state nor senior officials showed any appetite for handing over even modest transport powers to the proposed new assemblies (see Chapter Seven for further discussion on this).

A significant issue over the devolution of transport powers to the mayor did arise later in the process of establishing the GLA, over the proposed public-private partnership for the refurbishment of the London Underground. But, in this instance, the source of resistance was predominantly the Treasury, reflecting Gordon Brown's personal antipathy to Ken Livingstone, who was emerging as a strong potential candidate to win the London mayoralty. As a back-bench MP Livingstone had repeatedly criticised Gordon Brown's economic policies, and even called publicly for his dismissal. As Livingstone was implacably opposed to the public-private partnership approach, which he described as 'privatisation', the Chancellor was reluctant to allow Livingstone, if elected mayor, the power to scrap the partnership. The Treasury also remained nervous about the risk of repeating the unhappy experience of serious cost overruns, as had occurred on the last major London Underground project, the Jubilee Line extension in the late 1990s. This aside, the process of devolving a comprehensive package of transport powers to the mayor was not particularly problematic. Indeed one of the powers specifically provided for was the possible introduction of congestion charging in London. This made it possible for Ken Livingstone to introduce the Central London Congestion Charge without having to seek prior approval from the electorate, which proved an insurmountable obstacle in other cities, such as Greater Manchester, which were also interested in the possibility.

With policing there were more complex issues. In part this reflected the long and tortuous history of the Metropolitan Police from its early 19th-century origins. From the outset its lines of accountability were to the Home Secretary, and the Home Office was not keen to surrender its influence. But this was not just defending the status quo. The Met is more than the local police force for London. Its role embraces a number of national and strategic policing functions, including counter-terrorism, which justify a continuing line of accountability to central government. There is also the delicate issue of preventing inappropriate political influence in operational decisions, which remained sensitive following some of the bitter criticism of the Metropolitan Police by the GLC in the 1980s. All of these argued for some continuing central government oversight. But it was clearly wrong and unsustainable for London, alone of all areas of England, to have no line of democratic accountability for the performance of its local police force.

The solution we proposed, which was generally supported both by the police and other respondents to the Green Paper, was to create a new Metropolitan Police Authority along broadly similar lines to the then police authorities elsewhere in England, with a majority of its members being elected. Almost all of these would be members of the assembly. These would include the deputy mayor, who was expected to chair the new authority. While these structures have now been superseded, as have the former police authorities outside London, they did provide a broadly acceptable basis for extending democratic oversight for policing in London in the early years of the GLA. More problematic was the split responsibility for the appointment of the Metropolitan Police Commissioner, with the mayor having an influence but with the Home Secretary making the final recommendation (the Metropolitan Police Commissioner remaining a royal appointment). The tension over the departure in 2008 of Sir Ian Blair, who was effectively forced out of office by the incoming mayor, and the appointment of his successor highlighted the difficulties that inevitably flow from the Commissioner's essentially having two masters. While the Metropolitan Police continues to fulfil both a national and a local policing role, that tension is likely to remain.

In March 1998 a White Paper[2] was published setting out firm plans for the new authority that would be subject to a referendum in early May, on the same day as the London borough council elections. While we were bound to hold such a referendum as part of the wider devolution process, there was a further very powerful case for seeking the direct endorsement of the London electorate for our plans. In 1986 the GLC had been abolished by Act of Parliament without the people of London having the opportunity to say whether or not they agreed. This was a simple product of the supremacy of Parliament in the British constitution. A referendum giving clear public endorsement to the creation of a new London-wide authority would not of itself change that constitutional position but it would make it much harder psychologically for any future government to abolish the GLA without at the very least offering a further referendum on the issue. At the time, the Conservative Party was still opposed to the restoration of a democratic city-wide authority. It was therefore conceivable that, were it to return to government, it might seek to follow the Thatcher government's example. Making that more difficult and giving the new authority the legitimacy of clear public support was an important consideration.

The outcome was decisive. Not only did the referendum show a convincing (two to one) majority in favour; remarkably, that majority was reflected in every London borough. Even in Conservative bastions such as Bromley, an area renowned for its hostility to the GLC in the 1980s, a majority of local electors supported the creation of the GLA. This was not just a vindication of the policy, it was also, I believe, a key factor in prompting the Conservative Party to change its policy and accept the need for the new, democratic, city-wide authority. On the back of this referendum result, the legislation creating the new authority had a relatively straightforward passage through Parliament. Straightforward but not short. All the complex previous arrangements – covering each constituent part of the new authority – had to be repealed or amended. In the case of the Metropolitan Police this involved several hundred amendments/ repeals of measures dating back to the early 19th century. Indeed, when the Greater London Authority Bill was presented shortly before its introduction to the House of Commons, one of the officials responsible commented that he thought it was the longest piece of legislation since the 1936 Government of India Act. My reply was to hope that it lasted longer! I can now tell this story without trepidation.

One issue that did pose potential difficulties and presaged future divisions was the composition of the committee due to scrutinise the Bill in the House of Commons. Ken Livingstone, former GLC leader and by then a Brent MP, had expressed a wish to be a member of the committee, despite having made some characteristically provocative remarks about the Bill – he had described the proposed directly elected mayor as 'absolutely barmy'. The government Whips' Office, clearly worried about Ken's 'loose cannon' reputation, was inclined to exclude him from the committee, a view that I resisted. Given the size of the government's majority, there was no risk of the Bill's being derailed by one committee member even if he had chosen – which he did not – to vote against every clause. Common sense prevailed and he was appointed to the committee and played a constructive if surprisingly quiet role in the Bill's progress.

Once the legislation had completed its parliamentary passage, there were three further essential tasks to be done. First was the organisation of the election of mayor and assembly, scheduled for May 2000. As with the referendum, it was necessary to have a central body responsible for the overall administration and declaration of results, aggregating the returns that would come from the London boroughs. Given the size of the franchise, and the proportional systems applying separately to the mayoral and assembly elections, an electronic counting system was clearly essential to ensure a reasonably prompt declaration of results. In the event, things did not go quite as planned. While working satisfactorily in all the 'test' counts arranged in advance, the counting machines proved problematic on the night. It turned out that micro-fibres from the green baize tablecloths deployed, purely for appearance' sake, in the real count (but not in the trials) were sucked into the counting machines, causing them to malfunction – a classic illustration of the capacity for things to go wrong despite apparently meticulous prior testing. Despite this glitch, the outcome was not adversely affected.

Second was the need to set up a 'shadow' administration to prepare the ground for the newly elected mayor and assembly. Without such arrangements the new authority would have been in office but without the means to operate effectively in the early months. Bob Chilton, a former local authority chief executive, took charge of this shadow administration and its work in the months leading up to the election of the new authority, making possible a smooth transition to the point where the mayor and assembly were able to assume and exercise their powers and functions. In turn, Anthony Mayer, former chief executive of the housing corporation, was appointed chief executive of the

GLA and oversaw its move into its new headquarters building and the first eight years of its existence.

The third task was to commission a building for the new authority. While it would have been possible to leave this to the new authority, albeit with some temporary accommodation being made available at the outset, we took the view that it would put unreasonable pressure on a new body, particularly one that had been designed to be lean and streamlined, to have to oversee the procurement of a new headquarters building in the early years, which probably, given planning and construction timetables, would not have been completed during the authority's first term. County Hall, which had been the GLC's headquarters, was not available – it had been sold by the Conservative government – and in any case its size and grandiose early 20th-century municipal style would have been totally unsuitable for the much smaller and strategic GLA.

To generate an appropriate and iconic home for the new authority we launched an open competition for the design and development of the new building, which attracted a range of options in terms of style, structure and location. The winning team, led by Ken Shuttleworth from Foster and Partners (now senior partner at MAKE) working with the developers of More London, came up with a highly innovative solution symbolically located opposite the Tower of London, on the South Bank and with views down river towards the development opportunities in East and South-East London, rather than reinforcing the dominance of Westminster as the centre of government in London. Ken Livingstone, who initially pejoratively described it as 'a glass testicle', subsequently on moving in sent me a generous note of 'thanks' for having provided him with a fitting home for the mayoralty. His only complaint was that it was too small. I responded by pointing out that this was deliberate, to discourage empire building! However, in truth one cannot constrain a democratically elected mayor, and Ken had the last laugh as both the remit of the GLA and its size have grown significantly beyond what we originally envisaged. For all that, City Hall has proved to be an iconic and well-used headquarters building for the new authority, and had the added benefit of being delivered on time and within budget.

Fifteen years on, in 2015, what is the verdict on the GLA? There can be no question that the mayor has become a well-established and powerful force in London and the likelihood of a repeat of the 1986 abolition of London's city-wide government is very remote indeed. The post has attracted colourful and high-profile mayors who have stamped their personality, for better or worse, on London government. The first two mayors, Ken Livingstone and Boris Johnson, both won second terms, which gave a remarkable degree of consistency in the formative years of the new institution The highly visible mayoralty has not just been good for democracy, it has also delivered a number of very significant advances for London, including major infrastructure investment such as Crossrail, and of course the 2012 Olympics. London's economy has been buoyant for almost the whole period since the GLA came into existence. Despite the shock of the 2008 credit crunch, recovery came much faster and firmer in London than in most other parts of the UK. Furthermore, London's population has been growing by leaps and bounds, and with substantial overseas investment pouring in this trend is likely to continue. While government support was of course essential to delivering many of these outcomes, it is precisely because London has a high-profile mayor, able to influence decision makers at national and international level, that political support has been forthcoming for such major ventures. Arguably, London has achieved a significant advantage vis-à-vis other British cities through having an influential regional voice that no other areas in England have been able to match. This poses interesting questions to which we shall return in the next chapter.

The GLA has been innovative in promoting solutions to problems such as traffic congestion and air pollution, although there is still a long way to go on both. It has also been effective in advancing the case for further devolution, securing an increase in its housing and planning powers in 2008 and promoting the case for further fiscal devolution in 2013.[3]

Less successful, perhaps, has been the relationship between the mayor and the assembly. The latter has from the outset been relatively uncomfortable about being limited to a predominantly scrutinising function, although this was always the nature of the assembly's role. Having said that, the balance that was from the outset built into the budgetary process, allowing the assembly to override the mayor, but only if it secures a two-thirds majority, has worked, in that the authority has never been deadlocked – a risk that has adversely affected several American mayoral governance models on a regular basis. The assembly would obviously in principle favour a less demanding threshold, but, were the mayor's powers to be further restricted, this could well lead to less effective and less bold government than we have seen during the first 15 years of its existence.

When the GLA was being set up, some commentators, such as Simon Jenkins,[4] argued that it had not been given sufficient powers and was still too beholden to central government. While the argument can always be advanced for further devolution – and the GLA has voiced its view very effectively – in reality the two mayors of London over the period from 2000 to 2016 have proved the ability of the post to influence outcomes far beyond the formal remit of the GLA. Sub-national government has benefited significantly from this process, and the forces of centralisation have been notably reversed. Why this has not happened to the same degree in the rest of England is the question to which we should now turn.

SEVEN

The long and winding road to devolution in England

London is one of nine defined English regions. With its new, city-wide authority established from spring 2000, and proving popular and successful, the question obviously arose as to whether other English regions should also enjoy the benefits of devolved powers. The case for devolution to the English regions was given added impetus both by the successful devolution of powers to Scotland and Wales and by the long-standing commitment of John Prescott. While in opposition before the election victory of 1997, he had commissioned work on the case for regional authorities in England, broadly following the European model where regional tiers of government are widespread and generally seen to be effective. Indeed, among the various European regional government models the German Länder, put in place largely at British instigation in the aftermath of the Second World War as a counter to the re-emergence of an over-mighty national German state, were seen as among the most successful models of sub-national governance in Europe. In the 1997–2001 Parliament, John Prescott's department had overseen both the creation of the GLA and the introduction of Regional Development Agencies (RDAs) to promote economic growth and development in all English regions. Following the 2001 general election, when he was initially in charge of the Cabinet Office (although in summer 2002 he returned to his former department, now renamed the Office of the Deputy Prime Minister – ODPM) he gave a clear steer that one of his top priorities was the extension of regional devolution in England.

The 2001 Labour Party manifesto had made a commitment to offer the opportunity of a devolved regional assembly in those English regions that demonstrated support for it through a referendum. This recognised that the appetite for regional devolution varied from area to area. Indeed, in some parts of the country there was little sense of regional identity. The South East, for example, covered a wide range of counties, both north and south of London, extending from Kent at one end to Buckinghamshire at the other. Apart from their proximity to London, there were few common interests across such a diverse area to suggest a need for them to have a single regional assembly. Other parts of England, particularly in the North, felt stronger common bonds. This made it difficult, if not impossible, to devise a devolution framework which would appeal in all areas. While this might suggest the case for a review of the regional boundaries, the exercise would inevitably have taken years to conduct, and it would not necessarily have produced boundaries that would have proved any more popular or practical. In Cornwall, for example, there was a powerful lobby that wanted the county to be designated as a region in its own right, and not as part of a South West region.

This made it inevitable that the proposals for regional devolution developed in 2002–03 would be optional rather than prescriptive, and an asymmetric outcome was expected, with some regions opting for devolved powers and others not. The more optimistic members of the team tasked with developing the devolution proposals hoped that a successful introduction of regional assemblies in some regions would generate momentum, leading others to follow as they saw benefits accruing to the pioneers from having significant powers devolved for local decision. But that, of course, depended on a convincing package of powers that would make sense in both constitutional and economic terms.

There was already the precedent in London of an intermediate body, sitting between central government and local authorities. As we saw in Chapter Six, the GLA's powers had been designed to cover those strategic functions that were better determined at a London-wide level, while local service delivery remained with the borough councils. The logic for this division was strong.

Whether in London or in regions outside the capital, transport, strategic planning and economic development objectives are best defined and managed at a level that covers a wider area than that governed by individual local authorities. Some other policy issues such as environmental oversight and culture have both local and wider regional dimensions. The distinction is not always easy to prescribe. Refuse collection, for example, is generally best managed locally, but waste disposal requires a wider perspective, and issues such as air quality can only be properly managed across a broader canvass.

John Major's government had, in the early 1990s, recognised the need for better regional coordination of a number of functions for which central government remained responsible, and had established government offices in each of the English regions for this purpose. But because they were outposts of Whitehall, and their lines of accountability were to ministers, there was an obvious democratic deficit, as there had been in London between the abolition of the GLC in 1986 and the election of the GLA in 2000. While many of the government offices in the regions had tried hard to build strong local links and reflect to Whitehall the needs and concerns of their respective regions, they were ultimately creatures of central government and were not seen by advocates of devolution as an adequate alternative to a body elected by and accountable to the people of their region. Similarly the chambers that had been set up at the same time as RDAs to provide a degree of democratic oversight to the RDAs also lacked that direct line of accountability to the people of the region, as they were appointed by local authorities and business organisations. Directly elected regional assemblies were designed to fill this vacuum. In the words of the White Paper that set out the government proposals:

> Building on the success of devolution elsewhere in the UK, we believe that elected regional assemblies will be able to reduce bureaucracy and provide a new regional level of public scrutiny and democratic accountability. By taking powers from Whitehall and government quangos (not from local authorities) they will bring decision-making under closer democratic

control – offering people in the region a distinct political voice and a real say over decisions which matter to them, on issues such as jobs, transport, housing, culture and the environment.[1]

In keeping with the model that had been adopted in London, the White Paper put a strong emphasis on a lean and streamlined structure for the regional assemblies, with between 25 and 35 members (allowing for the variation in size between large regions such as the South West and North West, and smaller ones like the North East). It was also stipulated that where regions voted for regional assemblies, this should be accompanied by a move to unitary local government in that region, so that counties and districts would be replaced by unitary local authorities. This was already the pattern of local government in London, in most of the big cities and in some county areas, as well as in Scotland and Wales. The purpose of extending unitary local government was to avoid the creation of a fourth tier of government (national, regional, county and district) in areas with elected regional assemblies. While this helped to counter the claims of some critics that the creation of regional assemblies would involve a proliferation of politicians and bureaucracy, it did inevitably pose a threat to existing councillors in county and district councils, who would have seen their positions abolished in the consequent reorganisation.

The White Paper placed a strong emphasis on the importance of economic development in each region:

An effective regional policy is vital, both to tackle the historic regional disparities and to respond to the challenges of the modern knowledge economy. Central government has an important role to play in trying to increase growth across all regions. However history suggests that a centralist policy is not the best answer; too much intervention in the regions is as damaging for the whole country as too little interest in them. It is vital to give real economic power to the regions to enable them to improve regional prosperity.[2]

Regional devolution was therefore seen not just as a desirable objective in its own right but also as a means to promote regional growth and to empower representatives of the English regions to exercise much greater influence over the economic development of their region. There was encouragement for close working relations with business and for business involvement in the development of regional economic strategies, as well as an inclusive approach to the involvement of other stakeholders in the work of the regional assembly.

The White Paper made it clear that a referendum on whether or not an elected regional assembly should be set up would only be held in regions expressing an interest, so the government invited expressions of interest and undertook to hold soundings to establish whether or not there was sufficient interest in any single region to justify progressing to a referendum. While this was not necessarily a very scientific way of gauging the degree of public support for the proposition, it soon became clear that, in principle, support for the concept of an elected regional assembly was concentrated in the north of England. There were advocates of regional devolution in the South West, but a lack of agreement on what constituted the natural boundaries of the South West, together with the separatist instincts of many in Cornwall, made it impossible to present a specific proposal that was likely to command support in a referendum. Even within the three northern regions there were disparate voices, some simply opposed to the assembly concept, others preferring other models for devolution. In the North West, and particularly in Manchester, there was already a growing interest in the city-region model, and this had its advocates who preferred the concept of a Greater Manchester area with devolved powers to an elected regional assembly covering the wider North West region.

In the event, the conclusion of the government soundings was that only the North East had shown the degree of support necessary to justify holding a referendum. Accordingly the government introduced legislation to allow a referendum to be held in the North East region, and also asked the Boundary Commission to review the existing boundaries in the parts of the North East where two-tier local government still applied (Northumberland and Durham), with a view to making recommendations on a fully unitary structure for local government in the region. The referendum was scheduled to take place in late 2004, with the ballot (which was conducted by post) closing on 4 November. As with the procedure in respect of London, it was made clear that the detailed legislation to create a North East regional assembly would be introduced only if the referendum resulted in a 'Yes' vote. There were some arguments about whether or not there should be a threshold, in terms of the percentage of the electorate participating in the referendum, to validate the outcome, but these suggestions were rejected on the basis that devolution to Scotland had been deferred for 20 years as a consequence of the threshold inserted into the procedures for the referendum in the 1970s. Although the people of Scotland had voted 'Yes', the 40% threshold was not achieved, leaving a long-lingering sense of grievance north of the border that was remedied only in 1998. In the event, both the level of turnout (47.1%) and the margin of the result (77.9% against) were clearly more than sufficient to avoid any dispute arising in the absence of a defined threshold.[3]

The key question that does arise is why was there such a large majority against the proposed North East regional assembly. When the government White Paper was published in summer 2002, media coverage suggested that there would be little support for the proposal in several parts of the country, particularly in the South, but there was a widely held assumption that there was a real appetite for regional devolution in the North, most notably in the North East. Until the later stages of the referendum campaign, when a 'No' vote began to be seen as not just possible but likely, it was generally assumed that the North East would vote for a regional assembly. What accounts for the about-turn? I believe there are four main explanations, of which the first is by far the most significant.

1. *Inadequate powers.* The 'No' campaign made great play during the referendum campaign of an inflatable white elephant, symbolising its view that the North East regional assembly would be a 'talking shop' with few powers. This did not just catch the public fancy, but reflected a hard truth. Most of the powers that the government proposed devolving to the North

East regional assembly were tightly constrained. Whereas in London the mayor, through the new delivery agency TfL, took over responsibility for all main transport services other than aviation, the North East assembly would have enjoyed only a limited say and virtually no control over transport matters. The assembly's powers would have extended to little more than advising the government on the allocation of transport funding within the region, and making proposals to the Highways Agency and the (then) Strategic Rail Authority on new investment priorities. In all cases the final decision would remain with Whitehall. This crudely reflected the reluctance of the Department of Transport to hand over powers to the assembly. In 1997, when the GLA was being created, officials in the transport team within the DETR, were not always keen to see powers given to the mayor and TfL, but John Prescott as Secretary of State was able to insist on the devolution, and indeed did. In 2002–03 transport was now in a separate department, and the new Secretary of State, Alastair Darling, although polite, was frankly hostile to giving away powers he had only recently taken over.

As a result, those campaigning for a 'Yes' vote in the referendum were vulnerable to questions highlighting its limited authority. In the course of several meetings in the region over the summer and autumn of 2004, I was repeatedly asked if the assembly would be able to take forward plans to improve the A1 north of Newcastle-upon-Tyne with dual carriageway all the way to Scotland. This was seen by many in Northumberland, and more widely in the North East, as a high priority to improve communications and road safety, but in response I could only say that the assembly would be in a strong position to lobby for this improvement. It wasn't a reply likely to win support among the sceptics, but it was the truth. Similar parallel questions could be and were asked about the limited powers of the assembly in other policy areas. The cumulative effect over the course of the referendum campaign was to validate the critique of the 'No' campaign that the assembly would be a toothless talking shop and a waste of money. I have no doubt that this was the key influence explaining the erosion of support for the proposed assembly and the decisive 'No' vote. Some people have pointed out that there was criticism of the proposed GLA and London mayor proposal in 1998 on the grounds that the powers of the new authority were insufficient.[4] However, the GLA had substantial powers over transport and policing, both of which were seen as key issues in London. By contrast, the elected regional assembly had no power over policing, and only a modest influence over transport. The contrast was stark.

2. *Lack of cross-government support.* The reluctance of other government departments to cede powers to the proposed regional assemblies was symptomatic of a wider lack of support for the devolution proposals. While Tony Blair had been strongly supportive of the creation of the mayor of London and the GLA he was perceived to be much less enthusiastic for the creation of regional assemblies elsewhere, and while he did make one visit to the North East to support the 'Yes' campaign during the referendum, this was thought to reflect a sense of obligation to the Deputy Prime Minister rather than his own conviction. Other senior members of the government were similarly at best lukewarm in support for regional assemblies. Some were frankly hostile. The whole agenda was often presented as John Prescott's personal commitment to the North and to the European model of regional devolution. This inevitably coloured the way in which the proposed regional assembly was perceived by many commentators, and probably contributed to the erosion of confidence in the proposed assembly model.

3. *Timing.* Almost every local representative in the North East to whom I spoke about the reason for the 'No' vote felt that the proposal would have had a better prospect of success had it been presented five years earlier. All emphasised that there had been strong support in the region for the principle of devolution in the late 1990s, at the time when devolution to Scotland, Wales, Northern Ireland and London had been progressing, but the passage of time had taken its toll. The government itself had become less popular than it had been in the wake of its 1997 election triumph. The Iraq War in 2003 had further eroded support from those who might have been expected to support the government's proposal.

Additionally, the very nature of a referendum, which allows electors to express their view without leading to a change of government, made the proposition vulnerable, as it gave an easy opportunity for traditional Labour supporters to cast a protest vote without this leading to the loss of the Labour government. As the North East is a region that traditionally has been strongly Labour in its voting preferences, this may well have been a factor contributing to the disproportionately large majority by which the government's proposal was rejected.

A further factor, which may on the surface appear contradictory, is that in the seven years that the Labour government had been in power there had been demonstrable advances in the North East in urban regeneration, investment and economic development. The transformation of the river Tyne, flowing between Newcastle and Gateshead, with the development of two major new cultural centres, the Baltic mill reopening as a centre for visual arts and the Sage concert hall, both on the Gateshead side, together with the iconic pedestrian bridge across the river and a plethora of new bars, restaurants and hotels as well as offices and commercial centres along the Newcastle waterfront, was a powerful symbol of economic recovery. The case for regional devolution as a means of securing improvements in the local economy may well have appeared less convincing in 2004, as many of those improvements appeared to be coming without the elected regional assembly. I doubt that this would have been a persuasive argument if the proposed assembly had a relevant and convincing range of powers, but without them there was an understandable basis for questioning whether there was any real need for it.

4. *Turkeys don't vote for Christmas.* The local government reorganisation which was integral to the proposal involved the abolition of two-tier local government in Northumberland and Durham. Two county councils and 13 district councils would be replaced by either two or, at most, five unitary councils. This meant that a large number of local councillors would lose their job, status and financial allowances as a result of a 'Yes' vote. Hardly surprisingly, this dampened their enthusiasm for the proposal. As this group of people included a substantial

number of opinion shapers in local communities, it made it harder for the advocates of an elected regional assembly to build broad-based support for the 'Yes' vote. By contrast with London, where there had been overwhelming support from the capital's political leadership for the creation of the GLA, in the North East local political voices were divided, and this unquestionably undermined the 'Yes' campaign. The issue of local government reorganisation was in practice a difficult one to resolve satisfactorily, for without it the elected regional assembly proposal would have been vulnerable to the charge that it was creating yet another tier of politicians. The issue hadn't arisen in London, where local government was already reorganised on a unitary basis. Grasping it in the North East was bound to alienate a substantial number of local opinion formers who otherwise were likely to have been more positive about the elected regional assembly proposal. Ironically, they gained little from the 'No' vote, as the outcome within a short period of time was a move to unitary local government across both Northumberland and Durham.

One of the ironies of the process was that, in parallel with the proposed regional devolution policy, the government was also promoting a devolution package for local government. The policies, set out in the 2001 White Paper, 'Strong local leadership; quality public services', and enacted in the 2003 Local Government Act, offered a significant number of new powers to local government. These included the lifting of borrowing controls imposed by the Thatcher government and their replacement with a prudential borrowing regime, allowing greater freedom to borrow in order to finance necessary investment; the introduction of a power to trade as well as powers to charge for discretionary services; powers to limit the Council Tax discount on second homes; a reduction in the number of reporting obligations imposed on local authorities; and the repeal of the much-hated Section 28 provision against the supposed 'promotion' of homosexuality − another relic of the Thatcher-era prejudices. Perhaps it was simply a reflection of the way government works, with different policies usually developed in silos and links not made as well as they could be between parallel themes, but the opportunity to present both regional and local devolution measures together, as a clear commitment from government to hand down powers, was not taken. Given the other factors working against the regional devolution agenda, this would probably not have made a significant difference, but it could have countered some of the negativity within local government ranks about the elected regional assembly proposal.

Before the referendum on the North-East regional assembly, the government had made it clear that without a majority in favour there would not be an elected regional assembly. The scale of the 'No' majority made this outcome all the more certain. In theory there could have been a further referendum in another region at a later date, but, given the margin of the vote against elected regional assemblies in the region thought most likely to be favourable, there was no question of trying again elsewhere. This of course left the whole issue of devolution in England hanging in the air. It was not, however, an issue that could be ignored indefinitely. The absence of devolved strategic powers across the whole of England, apart from London, stood in stark contrast to the already substantial, and soon to be extended, devolved powers in Scotland, Wales and Northern Ireland. The specific model of devolution proposed may have been rejected, but few people saw the outcome of the North East referendum as a vote against the principle of greater devolution in England. There was not, however, an obvious alternative. While the development of the city-region model looked the most promising way forward, this depended on cooperation between different local authorities in the metropolitan conurbations. In the later years of the Labour government, new legislation was introduced to facilitate closer working between different authorities and the creation of combined authorities. But this was not extensively adopted. Only in the Greater Manchester area was there any significant move towards such cross-authority cooperation, and it was still very early days for AGMA (the Association of Greater Manchester Authorities). Quite apart from this consideration, there was the inherent question of what was to happen in those (not insubstantial) parts of England not covered by city-regions.

The one clear advantage of a model built on the existing defined English regions was that it covered the whole country, so no areas would be left out. But if, following the North-East referendum, this was no longer a feasible option, alternatives would have to be developed that could offer the prospect of devolution to different parts of England, including the rural shire counties and non-metropolitan areas. Here there was an inevitable tension between the views of individual local authorities, most of which would have preferred greater direct devolution, without any over-arching regional or sub-regional body, and the powerful economic case for wider agglomeration across local authority boundaries if powers relating to transport, planning, economic development and other strategic services were to be devolved.

The return of the Coalition government in 2010 appeared to signal the end of the road for the defined English regions, even though it had been the Conservative government of John Major that had established the government offices in each region, and the Lib Dems had been strong supporters of the concept of regional devolution. The very word 'region' was anathema to the Conservative Secretary of State Eric Pickles, and his obvious antipathy to even discussing regional matters led to jokes around the DCLG about bodies called TAFKARs (Those Areas Formerly Known as Regions). Even the production of regional-based statistics was discontinued. With such a clear block to any further consideration of regionally based devolution, it became increasingly clear that the city-region was the only option for further devolution. The case for devolving more powers from central government to the English cities was powerfully developed during the life of the Coalition government by a number of bodies bringing together academics, economists, business people and local authorities, including the City Finance Commission.[5] This in turn found an echo in the London Finance Commission,[6] which emphasised the scope for stimulating economic growth through further devolution of powers to the capital. Initially the Coalition government's response was largely rhetorical, with much talk of 'localism' but, in reality, the maintenance of heavily centralising policies. Even where a degree of devolution was agreed, as with the partial localisation of Business Rates, the complexities of the scheme and the constraints still placed on local authorities made a mockery of the supposed freedoms being offered, let alone the incentive to promote economic growth. But the devolution genie could not be forced back into the bottle. The argument for devolution as a means to promote economic growth continued to be pressed. In the event, the progressive development of the collaborative model across the Greater Manchester area, and the persuasive case of the benefits to the sub-regional economy from greater devolution, made to Conservative Chancellor George Osborne by Manchester, won the day. To Osborne, an MP from that part of the country, acutely conscious of his political party's limited appeal in the North, the political attraction of being seen to be promoting a 'Northern powerhouse' was irresistible. So it seems likely that further devolution in the course of the 2015–20 Parliament will be focused on city-regions. To this extent the London model introduced in 2000 appears to be providing the template for the next phase of devolution to cities.

It is in one sense ironic that the metropolitan mayoral model of governance, introduced in London, has been pushed further forward as part of this process. While the people of London voted in 1998 in favour of an elected mayor responsible for city-wide government, only a very limited number of local areas across England showed any appetite for a mayoral governance model for their council. This was despite various efforts over the following 15 years by both the Labour and Coalition governments to promote wider adoption of the mayoral model. Indeed the option was very widely rejected by referenda held in a range of towns and cities from the late 1990s to 2012. The concept of directly elected executive mayors in local authorities has won support from different governments at Westminster over that period, but has been resisted by the large majority of local councillors, who preferred to stick with the model of an indirectly elected leader drawn from within their ranks. Even when central government has taken the option over the heads of local councillors and presented it to the electorate in local referenda, in most cases it has been turned down. Yet now, as a condition of devolving more powers to combinations of local authorities, the model of a directly elected executive metropolitan mayor appears to becoming acceptable at least to council leaders. As Simon Parker, director of the New Local Government Network, points out, the agreement of the Greater Manchester area council leaders to a directly elected mayor of their sub-region was purely theirs – a pragmatic decision taken by the political elite, but not endorsed or validated by the electorate. Just two years earlier the electors of Manchester city had rejected the proposal for an elected mayor when put to them in a referendum.[7] This poses an interesting question about the need for and importance of political leadership in promoting unpopular policies, a theme that has already been raised and will recur later in this book. It also highlights how long and tortuous a path has to be followed in order to make some policy initiatives acceptable and to translate them into practice.

EIGHT

The transformation
of Hackney

Hackney Council is today seen as a typical Inner London local authority, facing very significant challenges and responding well to the needs of its citizens in a range of policy areas. Its able and long-serving mayor, Jules Pipe, would not claim that it is perfect. Like any other public authority it can get things wrong from time to time, but he is justifiably proud of many of his council's achievements, and he has even more reason to be proud of the transformation of Hackney Council over a 15-year period. For it was not always like this. In summer 2001, when I was appointed Minister for Local Government, Hackney Council was widely seen to be in deep trouble. Its record in delivering most council services was abysmal. In its core responsibilities such as housing, social services, education, leisure services and street cleaning it was visibly failing. Perhaps even more telling was the extent to which many local residents had simply given up on getting any response, let alone positive action, from their council.

More than any other area in the country it was wallowing in a culture of excuses, attributing its dire performance standards to the poverty of its area and the claimed lack of government funding rather than to its own managerial incompetence. Yet, as became crystal clear within a few minutes of examining the brief I was given by my civil servants, the London Borough of Hackney was failing to collect no less than one-third of the Council Tax revenue owed to it.[1] While there was no doubt that Hackney was an area suffering from real poverty, the inability of the council to make use of the revenue to which it was entitled spoke volumes about its failure to rise to the admittedly serious challenges it faced. Nor was this just a short-term aberration. Hackney was known to have been plagued with problems for decades. Almost 20 years earlier in 1983 I had seen this at first hand, when invited by the then council leadership to advise Hackney on how to remedy its disastrous failure to administer the newly introduced Housing Benefit scheme. Although many other councils had faced difficulties with this challenge (see Chapter Three) Hackney was widely perceived to have been among the very worst in the country at that time. After a temporary improvement in performance in the 1980s, the problems recurred in the 1990s, together with the same sad symbol of administrative failure – a queue of desperate people forming each morning outside the council's benefits office, knowing that only a limited number would be seen each day. In an attempt to remedy the problem, the council had outsourced its revenue and benefit services, but without the necessary skills and structures to oversee the contract, it was perhaps not surprising that this failed to deliver an improvement. In the council's own words:

> In March 2001, the Revenues and Benefits service was being run by an outside contractor, ITNet, on behalf of the council. Service levels, as measured by Best Value Performance Indicators were some of the worst in the country. Many people had to wait up to 18 months to have their Housing Benefit claims assessed. Complaints were at a record level and long queues of clients were a daily occurrence.[2]

It was hardly surprising, given the absence of effective control, that suspicions of fraud and misappropriation of funds were widespread. An article in *Public Finance* magazine reported:

> Crisis ridden Hackney Council has launched a fraud investigation following the discovery of irregular cash transfers between bank accounts.... Finance managers at the authority have found that accounts were created and money transferred between them with no obvious explanation for the transactions.[3]

In the same month, a report from the recently appointed Acting Director of Finance and Performance revealed a conversation between Hackney Council and the then Department of Social Security (DSS) in which the Council had been advised that DSS lawyers had been looking at Hackney benefit payments and concluded that Housing Benefit determinations had not been properly made, so the council had no legal basis for making the payments of Housing Benefit that it had been issuing.[4]

It was hardly surprising that Hackney Council had attracted titles such as 'The worst run place in Britain'.[5] The Audit Commission summed up the state of the authority bluntly:

> Hackney is not a well-run council and has not been for too long ... The council has very serious financial problems and has not got them under control ...
>
> There is a culture of depressed cynicism amongst many of the council's management.
>
> We conclude that the council is not complying with its duty under Section 3 of the 1999 Act to make arrangements to secure continuous improvement in the way its functions are exercised ...[6]

This long-drawn-out saga of chaos, incompetence and failure raises awkward questions. First and most obvious is why the area's elected councillors failed to take effective action over such a long period of time to turn around a manifestly inadequate authority. Second, why did the democratic process fail to punish the councillors who presided over this mess and elect in their place a different set of local representatives who could transform the administration? Third, why did no one else intervene? Other local authorities knew only too well how bad the situation was in Hackney, and indeed were not slow to point out how the often-publicised failings of Hackney tarnished the overall reputation of local government. Fourth, why did central government not intervene? This last question was the one that I had to address. There were of course persuasive arguments against premature or capricious intervention by central government in the working of a separate tier of government with its own democratic legitimacy. During the 1980s the Thatcher government had unleashed an unprecedented series of interventions in the working of local government. Figure 8.1 graphically illustrates the story.

Figure 8.1: Major legislation affecting local government

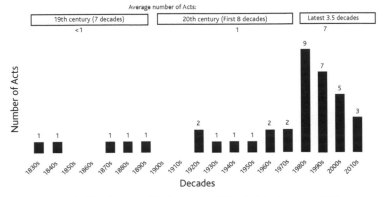

Source: N. Raynsford, 'Parliament and local government', Speaker's Lecture series 2014.

From the 1830s until the 1970s local government was affected by no more than one or two significant new pieces of legislation in any single decade. Indeed the average number was less than one per decade in the 19th century and only just over one in each of the first eight decades of the 20th century. Then everything changed. In the 1980s there were no fewer than nine significant new Acts of Parliament focused on local government, as many in that one decade alone as in the previous eight decades put together. Following this veritable flood of centralising measures, the tide has, as Figure 8.1 illustrates, begun to recede, but the process had rightly raised very significant questions about the role and independence of local government in England. Officials in the Department for Transport, Local Government and the Regions (DTLR), the government department responsible for the oversight of local government, were wary about directly intervening in the day-to-day running of a local authority. In part this was a view about constitutional proprieties, but it also reflected a natural caution against the risk of being sucked into a morass from which it might prove difficult to get out.

Partly as a result of such reservations, the department had placed its hopes on peer support, particularly from the IDeA (the Improvement and Development Agency), which was contracted to assist Hackney Council remedy its managerial and service delivery problems. The IDeA had conducted a peer review of Hackney in 1999, finding 'an almost complete absence of coherent political management' and serious financial mismanagement.[7] It had recommended a series of measures to improve performance, including the appointment of a managing director and the preparation of an improvement plan. But 18 months later it was clear that the authority was still in deep trouble. I was advised in June 2001, immediately after taking up my new ministerial role, that the council's director of finance and performance would probably be issuing a formal report in the coming week, under the provisions of the 1988 Local Government Finance Act (known as a Section 114 Report), indicating that the authority was effectively bankrupt and not capable of covering its expenditure. This would not have been the first time such a report had been issued. The previous October the then borough treasurer had been obliged by the new managing director, Max Caller, to issue such a report, and the council had been forced into agreeing a package of savings to reduce its deficit. But now, within only a few months, the council was facing an even worse financial crisis. While I understood the reluctance of government civil servants to intervene directly in Hackney, I did not feel it right simply to sit on the side-lines when confronted with such overwhelming evidence of the breakdown of normally accepted standards of administration.

This was the background to our decision in the summer of 2001 to serve directions on Hackney Council, using powers created in the 1999 Local Government Act, to ensure that the council faced up to its administrative and financial failings and put in place the necessary staff, policies and procedures to turn the authority's affairs around. Individual government departments had previously intervened in Hackney and other local authority areas in response to service failures in their area of interest. The Department for Education and Employment had done so in 1999 following a critical Ofsted Report, and the Department of Health had also intervened following an adverse inspection report on the council's children's services in the same year. But such interventions were not capable of remedying the endemic mismanagement across the whole of the council. At their best, they might lead to a temporary improvement in one service area. But they could equally have perverse consequences by focusing attention solely on that part of the organisation and diverting attention away from others where problems were just as severe. They also had the effect of reinforcing a silo mentality. This proved a real potential obstacle in Hackney, where the director of education was thought by the managing director to be prioritising her departmental interests over her obligations to the council, and so not adequately contributing to corporate recovery. In any case it was clear that without a more fundamental transformation in the council's overall management and financial control, we would be doing no more than putting sticking plasters on a life-threatening wound.

The two broad options open to the government were either to suspend the powers of the council, sending in a team of government appointees to take over the administration of the authority, or to issue directions requiring the council to act in specified ways. The first option would clearly be necessary, and indeed would be the only option, if it appeared that the council had no capacity or will to put in place an effective recovery programme even if instructed to do so. While some planning was undertaken in the department on this option (Plan B), our judgement was that the new leader of the council, Jules Pipe, and the managing director, Max Caller, had both the will and the ability to turn the council around, provided that they were given the necessary authority and obligations to enable them to impose solutions on a council that had previously proved reluctant if not incapable of doing the right thing. Jules Pipe had recently taken over the leadership of the council following a number of by-elections that had given the Labour Party an outright majority. Previously the council had been 'hung', with a joint Labour–Conservative administration notionally in power. While Pipe and the leader of the Conservative group, Eric Ollerenshaw, later to become an MP, had worked constructively together in that period, the lack of a majority administration had been seen as a further weakness, particularly in a local authority whose members from all parties had displayed an alarming degree of volatility on too many occasions. Indeed, in the previous winter the borough treasurer had been under huge pressure from councillors to prepare the next year's budget on an assumption of a 98% collection rate for Council Tax, when the council was collecting only around 65% and there was no realistic prospect of achieving the higher level. This volatility had seriously undermined the ability of previous administrations to drive through the tough but necessary programme of savings so as to deliver a realistic and balanced budget. Indeed it had reached the point where, between 1996 and 2000, there was no leader of the council and no formally approved administration. So, a great deal depended on Jules Pipe's ability to give the necessary leadership. He clearly recognised the dire state of the council and the need for drastic remedies. He was not therefore opposed to the imposition of government directions that would require the council to take the necessary steps to restore financial discipline and effective administration. Indeed he recognised that they would give him and Max Caller the backing to require agreement from other councillors to measures that they might otherwise have been unwilling to accept.

While the obligations in the directions were draconian, they were not simply imposed from above without consultation but had been discussed in advance with both Pipe and Caller. Both were just as determined as we were to achieve the necessary transformation, and so they were ready to go along with what was an unprecedented intervention. It was the first time that such powers had been deployed. In the following 15 years they were used on only a handful of occasions, most recently in Tower Hamlets in response to wilful mismanagement of that council by its mayor. In that case, the government also installed commissioners to take over control of the administration. In Hackney, the directions that were imposed in September 2001 were a joint initiative by five separate government departments.

1. The ODPM required Hackney:
   - to impose effective, sustainable budgetary and financial controls
   - to build managerial capacity
   - to improve service delivery capacity.

2. The Department for Health required Hackney to conduct a BestValue review of services for older people and for mental health.
3. The Department for Work and Pensions required Hackney to clear the outstanding benefit backlog.
4. DEFRA required Hackney to prepare a plan for operating waste management services.
5. The Department for Education and Skills required Hackney to establish a new body to take over responsibility for the management and delivery of education services in Hackney.

At the same time the ODPM appointed an engagement team to work with the council to ensure the implementation of a recovery programme and to monitor the council's compliance with the directions, as well as providing financial support to enable the authority to continue to operate. This was essential in a context where the S. 114 Report essentially put a block on the authority's incurring any further expenditure until there was a balanced budget in place.

From this point on, the Hackney story is one of recovery. Given the extent of the problems, it was inevitable that this would be a long, hard process, with several years of sustained effort required to turn around the council's performance and, indeed, its reputation. But evidence of progress began to be seen within a relatively short time. The budget-setting process in early 2002 was very different to that of a year earlier, when a large police presence at the town hall had been necessary to allow the councillors to meet, as the building had been surrounded by demonstrators against threatened cuts. Even so, the councillors had, in the managing director's words, to be forced to agree a legal budget and to reject proposed amendments that would have made it impossible to deliver.[8] A year later, he recalls walking peacefully and calmly across Mare Street with Jules Pipe prior to the meeting to approve the budget for 2002–03. By July 2002, Hackney was reporting that, after terminating the contract with ITNet and taking the service back in house, Council Tax collection rates had increased 'by six percentage points to 74%'. This was still by far and away the worst in the country, but at last was showing an improvement on previous levels. In September

2002 a new Education Trust had been set up as a partnership between an outside body and Hackney Council, and within a relatively short time school performance across the borough was showing a significant improvement. The district auditor, who had heavily criticised the authority's shortcomings up until 2001, took a very different line in his annual audit letter sent in January 2003:

> Hackney was the first council subject to intervention by government following severe overspends and a series of highly critical audit and inspection reports.
>
> Against this background the council has responded well and has met the requirements of the majority of the ministerial directions, and the green shoots of recovery are now starting to appear.
>
> However services are still mostly poor and much remains to be done if the improvements in underlying processes are to feed through into real changes for the residents of the Borough.[9]

This clear steer from the council's external auditor was helpful and welcome, confirming as it did the positive impact of the intervention without the potential downsides that some had feared. It also highlights the importance of a strong and confident external audit function, which has not always been in evidence in respect of local authorities in difficulty. Even if the external auditor is asking the right questions and rigorously examining all the evidence, troubling findings will not necessarily have the necessary impact if the political and officer leadership of the council seeks to side-line them and the auditor fails to press for remedial action.

There remained a lurking anxiety that the progress that was being made in Hackney could easily be derailed, particularly if there was an unexpected change in the political composition of the council at the local elections due in May 2002. I was very conscious of how important a role Jules Pipe had played in securing the commitment of the borough to the recovery plan. I was also conscious of how volatile Hackney politics had been over the previous decade or more, with frequent splits within party groups and equally frequent crossings of the floor from one party to another. This didn't just explain why Hackney's elected councillors had been unable to take the necessary steps to turn the council around. It also explained why the electorate had not been able to replace a failing administration with a better one, because it was difficult to know, in the confusion of shifting party allegiances, who was to blame.

Jules Pipe's election to the leadership had at last created a possibility of sustained commitment to reform. But if he were to lose his seat or be ousted from the leadership and the borough were to lapse back into the political instability that had allowed so much damage to be caused in the past, all the gains would be put at risk again. So, with a view to securing a strong mandate for Jules to carry through the recovery plan, I suggested that Hackney should consider adopting a mayoral system of governance. This was an option available to local authorities, and indeed had been considered by a Democratic Convention that had been convened in Hackney in 1998. Although the convention had recommended adoption of a mayoral constitution, this, along with many other reform initiatives, had failed to win majority support from the highly fragmented council of the time in which alliances could all too easily be formed to stop things happening.

If the possibility was now to be resurrected, it required backing from the local electorate in a referendum. Provided that this was secured, Pipe would be able to seek a four-year term as mayor from the Hackney electorate, and this I hoped would give him both the time and the authority to carry through the improvement programme to a point where backsliding would no longer be a serious risk. Although cautious, not least because he was unsure how this might affect his relations with his fellow councillors, Pipe understood the importance of maintaining the positive momentum that had been in evidence since autumn 2001 and agreed that the council should put the option of a mayoral constitution to the electorate in a referendum, to be held on the same day as the council elections in May 2002. Both delivered a vote of confidence. Pipe was re-elected as a councillor at the head of an enlarged Labour group with a workable majority over the other parties, and a majority also voted in favour of the adoption of a mayoral constitution. The election of Hackney's mayor followed in the autumn, with Pipe securing the post comfortably and so consolidating the prospects of successfully transforming the borough.

Four years later, early in 2006, after I had left government, the ODPM was able to write to Hackney to confirm that government engagement was ended. The report to the responsible minister, Jim Fitzpatrick, charted the improvement process over the intervening years and confirmed that by 2005 all the council's basic services were assessed as safe and improving, adding 'no school is in special measures – a major milestone'.[10]

What were the key factors in this remarkable turnaround, and what lessons can be learned about raising performance standards more widely? There were, in my view, four principal elements that together accounted for the successful turnaround in Hackney, and there are several important lessons that were carried across into the wider local government improvement agenda with which I was also closely involved. The four elements were:

1. *Local acknowledgement of the scale of the problem.* After years of denial and a seemingly endless stream of excuses for under-performance, Hackney acknowledged from 2001 onwards that the key problem was the council's own dysfunctional behaviour. The solution therefore lay in the council's own hands, and required an honest recognition that the way in which it had previously organised its business, taken (and then often countermanded) decisions and managed its staff was not just inappropriate but had contributed substantially to the mess the council found itself in. So too had been its unwillingness to listen to past warnings issued by the district auditor, and the inappropriate pressure put on senior officers by councillors to agree unrealistic estimates and unachievable budgets. Putting those problems right required the courage to disown much in the culture of the organization, which had become engrained and had been transmitted from one cohort of councillors to another over a period of several years. The election of Jules Pipe to the leadership (initially the joint leadership) of the council was a crucial moment as he, together with a significant number of younger, recently elected councillors, recognised that there had to be a dramatic

change in the culture of the council if it was to break out of the cycle of under-performance, excuses and failure into which it had become locked. It was for me refreshing to be dealing with political leaders willing to put their hands up and admit to the severity of the problems, rather than, as happens too often, seeking to minimise or make excuses for the failure.

2. *Effective collaboration between the council's political and officer leadership.* The close bond of confidence and trust between Jules Pipe and Max Caller was fundamental to the success of the recovery programme. Each recognised and respected the other's role, and the two worked together effectively to deliver the recovery programme and meet the requirements of the government directions. By doing so they were able to prevent wedges being driven between them by those with an interest in frustrating their agenda. These included disaffected councillors who wished to cling to the old way of doing things, some of the trade unions who saw both the leader and managing director as a threat and some community organisations that did not want to lose the privileged access they felt they had to the council under the old regime. As all of these groups, if they had got their way, would have prevented the council from changing for the better, it was vital that the link between the councillor and officer leadership remained strong, and both were united in their objectives and working methods. Each in turn had to maintain the loyalty and support of their own close confidantes, the councillor colleagues who had elected Pipe as their leader and the senior officers brought in by Max Caller to transform the organisation's performance and culture.

3. *Getting the fundamentals right.* The absence of adequate management and financial controls explained how Hackney, prior to 2001, was unable to set or adhere to a realistic and balanced budget. There was no effective management accounting, so overspending was not identified until long after the event. Individual departments and sections of the council often saw themselves as semi-autonomous units and, as such, were vulnerable to pressures coming from a range of sources outside the normal chain of command. So, high on the managing director's priorities was getting appropriate controls

in place to ensure that resources were properly allocated to approved purposes, expenditure was closely monitored and the expected outcomes were delivered. This required both systems and reliable personnel. Given the demoralised state of the authority, bringing in new blood was vital, and both the ODPM and the wider local government community in London were able to help Max Caller to secure the necessary staff. In the early days it called for particularly resolute and tough individuals who had to impose controls and order on an organisation that had in many areas ceased to show the appropriate degree of respect for such obligations. In the past Hackney had seen many well-intentioned staff lose heart and leave, faced with seemingly insurmountable obstacles. So, one of the key tasks was to build a cadre of trustworthy and capable senior officers who could together deliver the necessary change in the organisation's culture. This also required a corporate commitment to improvement across all parts of the authority, rather than the silo-based approach that had previously been allowed to develop in various parts of the council.

4. *Government intervention, engagement and support.* The directions issued in autumn 2001 were a watershed. There had previously been several claimed new starts for Hackney, but none had succeeded in transforming the council's deeply embedded culture of under-performance. This time it worked, for the reasons outlined above and because government had clearly signalled that things had to change and had imposed a series of obligations on the council that required sustained commitment to the recovery plan. This was, however, more than just a diktat from on high. There was close and continuing contact at both political and officer level, and significant financial support. This gave confidence to the council's political and officer leaders that they would not be left on their own, nor would their task be made more difficult by unco-ordinated demands for action from different government departments to tackle specific problems in silos, nor would they be subject to continual sniping and criticism for the authority's continuing poor performance. Inevitably it took time to achieve substantial improvements in many areas, so the council was rated 'poor' by the Audit Commission when

the first Comprehensive Performance Assessments were issued towards the end of 2002. Against this background Hackney's political and officer leadership were keen to highlight the evidence that things were getting better, even if there was still a long way to go. The ODPM, which had replaced the DTLR in summer 2002 as the responsible department, was happy to reinforce this message and to offer tangible demonstrations of its belief that the council's direction of travel was a positive one. When I asked Max Caller when he had felt confident that the council had turned the corner, his reply was 'the day you came to present the Investors in People Awards to Hackney staff, because although it was only a small thing it clearly indicated government's confidence in our progress. No minister would have come if they did not believe things were improving.'

The recovery of Hackney was just getting underway at the time that the government launched its 2001 Local Government White Paper. Entitled 'Strong local leadership; quality public services', the White Paper set out a series of measures designed to help local authorities better meet the expectations of their local communities. As its title indicated, the role of local authorities in giving leadership to their local communities was at the heart of the White Paper. The government signalled its intention to move away from the over-bureaucratic and over-prescriptive Best Value regime that had characterised its first term, and proposed to extend a number of new 'freedoms and flexibilities' to local government. This would involve giving greater discretion to councils in a number of areas, some of which have already been mentioned in Chapter Seven, including the exemption of the highest-performing authorities from 'Council Tax capping'. At the same time it introduced a new, more sharply focused performance management system to give every local authority a thorough assessment of its performance and to incentivise improvement. This 'Comprehensive Performance Assessment' (CPA) was to be developed and overseen by the Audit Commission, which was at the time struggling to find an appropriate successor to the Best Value regime with a stronger focus on corporate capacity rather than undue reliance on a plethora of service inspections.

The combination of the two major pillars of the White Paper, the freedoms and flexibilities on the one hand and the CPA on the other, was not accidental. We understood the importance of freeing local councils from some of the most burdensome restrictions that had been introduced by the Thatcher government and mainly remained in place subsequently, and also understood that if local authorities were to serve the interests of their communities they must have greater discretion to shape local partnerships and services. At the same time we wanted to demonstrate, partly to sceptical MPs, the extent to which local government had improved and was continuing to improve the quality of its service delivery. We were equally keen to exorcise the ghosts of the 1980s – a period of bitter conflict between local authorities and the government. That era had left a long shadow over the reputation of local government, not least among many MPs who had been cutting their political teeth at that time. In my judgement it was vital to provide unimpeachable evidence of the continuing improvement of local government performance if we were to win political backing for further reductions in central controls and the extension of greater freedom and discretion to local authorities.

Although, like many such performance measurement systems, CPA had a limited shelf life, it did have a very positive impact. After initial scepticism about the process, most local authorities recognised its value to them as a performance management tool and a way of demonstrating how well many of their services were being delivered.[11] The Audit Commission had, with our encouragement, gone out of its way to involve local government representatives in the design of the system, so that by the time it was launched much of the initial scepticism had evaporated. Nick Timmins, the highly respected public policy editor of the *Financial Times*, gave a remarkably positive assessment:

> What was the best thing about the Audit Commission's mighty assessment of the performance of local authorities published just before Christmas? Answer: it was a stunningly slim document which, in a mere

18 pages, allowed not just the local government anoraks but average citizens to see where their council stood, both locally and in relation to others. For those who have tangled with the mighty weight of performance indicators that the Commission has used in the past to measure service performance – hundreds of pages of the things – this was a distinct form of light among the darkness.

From a mass of data … came a clear and simple picture. The results, needless to say, have not avoided controversy … But what, nonetheless, has made the process sing is that rather than just measure service quality and customer satisfaction, the CPA has included an assessment of each council's capacity to improve. And that judgement has been applied as much to the politicians' ability to run the council as it has to the senior officers.

It might be thought that nothing could be more controversial. The whole point of elections, after all, is that if you don't like this lot you can throw them out and put the other lot in to see if they can do a better job.

But the brute truth of local politics is that there are parts of the country that for decades have been controlled by one party. The real power struggles have been within parties rather than between them, giving the electorate no say in who runs their local services.

And strangely enough – despite the acute nervousness in local government in the run-up to the publication of the results – local politicians appear in the main to have accepted, in a surprisingly grown-up way, that the question of how well they perform is not an unfair one to ask.[12]

Over the following years I noted how many local authorities started drawing on and quoting CPA evidence to show how well they were doing. Indeed, over its first few years the CPA provided powerful evidence of continuing improvement in the performance of most local authorities and of a very significant reduction in the numbers of councils facing serious challenges. Whereas the 2002 CPA assessment had revealed 23 upper-tier authorities in the two lowest categories ('Poor' and 'Weak'), the number was down to 7 by 2005 and to just 3 by 2008. This was despite a change introduced in 2005, making the test harder. The improvement in Hackney (which had been assessed as 'Poor' in 2002, and still 'Poor but improving strongly' in 2003 but by 2008 had reached a 3-star rating under the revised methodology) was mirrored in a number of other troubled authorities where similar engagement policies had been adopted to help them address their problems. Indeed the evidence that came out of the CPA reports very much reinforced the lessons that we had begun to learn from the intervention in Hackney and the engagement of government with other 'poor' and 'weak' authorities. Local ownership of the improvement process, good working relationships between political and officer leaders, getting the basics right with sound budgeting and good management systems as well as a strong sense of commitment to corporate goals, and the avoidance of rigid silos; all of these emerged from the CPA as clearly as from our engagement in Hackney as key factors contributing to an improvement in performance and the delivery of high-quality services.

One of the risks with all performance monitoring systems is that as the methodology becomes more familiar through regular use, the scope for 'gaming' the system grows. The attention of those whose performance is being measured can then shift, whether deliberately or not, from seeking to improve outcomes to a focus on improving those indicators that most influence the assessment of performance. Frequent changes in the methodology may help to counter this tendency, but they also have downsides. First, they make it less easy to measure progress over time, because changes, whether upwards or downwards, may simply reflect differences in methodology rather than actual performance. Second, they may, through seeking to include additional elements in order to give a more comprehensive picture, blur the clarity of the assessment. This is what happened to CPA. While there were perfectly valid reasons to extend the net by moving to a Comprehensive Area Assessment, looking more widely at the performance of all public services within the area (a move that fitted well with the emerging 'Total Place' agenda of 2009–10), it was difficult to hold a local authority to account for the performance of its partners delivering other public services in the area.[13] In all events, it, as well as the Audit Commission, fell victim to the incoming Coalition government's austerity budget and cull of quangos in 2010. It had run its course, but had played a significant role in encouraging real improvements in local government performance in the first decade of the 21st century.

While the evidence of such improvements across a range of local authorities was helpful in countering some of the lingering doubts felt in Westminster about local government, the case for following up with further devolution and relaxation of controls was dealt a serious blow by an unanticipated development just a few months after the first CPA results were made public at the end of 2002. In the early months of 2003 it became clear that the average increases in Council Tax demands being issued by local authorities in England were likely to reach double figures and would be significantly higher than in the previous year. To add to the concern, it also became clear that some of the largest increases were coming from councils that had been given the highest rating under the CPA system and accordingly had been promised exemption from Council Tax capping in the 2001 White Paper. The most egregious example was Wandsworth, which, having cut its Council Tax demand by 25% in 2002, which happened to be an election year, imposed a massive 57% increase in 2003.[14] While the Audit Commission's assessment of the 2003 Council Tax increases found no direct correlation between the level of Council Tax increase in individual authorities and that council's CPA rating, there was no doubt in my mind that local government as a whole had seen an opportunity to seek steep increases in Council Tax demands against the background of government pledges to relax the capping regime. With considerable public protest and deep unhappiness in 10 Downing Street about the average 12.9% increase in Council Tax that spring, it was inevitable that the pledged easing of the capping regime was withdrawn the following year. However, despite this setback and other disappointments at not having achieved all that I had hoped over my four years as Local Government Minister, I left office in 2005 knowing that there had been significant advances over those years in the performance and capacity of local government in England, and that Hackney Council was well on the road back from the margins to the mainstream.

NINE

'This won't take much of your time'

'This won't take much of your time. The policy is benign neglect.' With these remarkable and ill-timed words, Home Office officials handed over responsibility for the Fire Service to DTLR in 2001. This was one in a series of 'machinery of government' changes made following the 2001 general election. The rationale appears to have been the synergy between the administration and governance of the Fire Service and that of local government, but contemporary commentators were not necessarily convinced. 'Home Office loses Foxhunting and Fire' was the *Daily Telegraph*'s take on the process. In my experience, 'machinery of government' changes rarely achieve the expected benefits that they are supposed to deliver, and all too often feel like short-term tinkering for primarily political reasons. The department in which I served eight years as a minister had since 1970 been known as the Department of the Environment. In my time there it carried three different names, reflecting a series of 'machinery of government' changes. In 1997 it was expanded and renamed Department for the Environment, Transport and the Regions. In 2001 it was partially slimmed down and renamed Department for Transport, Local Government and the Regions (DTLR), and a year later was further slimmed down and renamed Office of the Deputy Prime Minister (ODPM). But that wasn't the end of the story. The department is now called the Department for Communities and Local Government, and is focusing on much the same priorities as the former Ministry of Housing and Local Government back in the 1960s. Indeed, responsibility for the Fire and Rescue Service has now been transferred back to the Home Office. I am far from convinced that much has been gained from these frequent changes of title, logo and responsibilities over the years. Indeed I have already alluded in Chapter Five to the downside consequences of the dismantling of the department's former construction sponsorship role.

However, the transfer of responsibility for the Fire Service to DTLR in 2001 is a more interesting example because this was not simply a shuffling of titular responsibility without any significant and lasting consequences. It proved more significant because it coincided with some profound changes in the way the service operates and in the outcomes of its work, and, as I will try to demonstrate, the change of departmental responsibility for the service was a significant influence on the process. In part these changes were prompted by external forces, most significantly the large pay claim submitted by the Fire Brigades Union (FBU) in 2002 and the consequent industrial dispute. This was on the cards irrespective of the 'machinery of government' change, but the transfer of responsibility resulted in a different set of ministers and officials having to deal with the many issues thrown up by the dispute, and those new sets of eyes brought new perspectives. The ability to see some of the issues afresh without preconceptions and free from accumulated corporate assumptions was a significant factor.

On reading the briefs prepared for me as the responsible minister, it was immediately clear to me that while there had been huge changes in the nature of the risks confronting the service since the 1940s, and equally far-reaching changes in the context within which it was operating, much of the disposition and ethos of the service remained rooted in legislation and doctrines that had been put in place in the immediate post-war era. Indeed the Act of Parliament that defined the duties and obligations of the Fire Service dated back to 1947 and had changed the governance arrangements from the war-time national fire service to one controlled by local authorities. Fire stations in most urban areas were heavily concentrated in former predominantly industrial, inner-city locations where, at that time, serious fires were most likely to occur and the main impact of war-time bombing had been felt. But, of course, over the subsequent half century much of the high-risk heavy industry had closed. At the same time, extensive suburban housing developments had dramatically changed the urban geography of Britain, with many more people living in more dispersed locations, not as immediately accessible as the streets of terraced housing in close vicinity to inner-city industrial centres. Not only had the location of fire stations remained heavily concentrated in areas much less likely to generate fires than had been the case 50 years before, but the service ethos remained very focused on putting out fires rather than preventing them. Firefighters had an admirable commitment to responding rapidly and bravely to incidents when they occurred, but far less emphasis had been given to stopping those fires occurring in the first place, or to making it easier for those affected to escape safely without the need for rescue. Indeed the funding formula used to allocate resources from government compounded the problem. By linking resource allocation to the number of call-outs in each fire authority area, the system acted as a disincentive to more effective preventive work, because a reduction in the number of fires, and therefore call-outs, would probably lead to a reduction in funding.

Not only was the funding system perverse in incentivising responding to fires rather than preventing them, but the statistics with which I was presented also told a disturbing story about the limits of what could be achieved within the prevailing framework and ethos. They showed that, tragically, around half of the people killed by fires in the home had already died before the alarm was raised. Most of such deaths were the result of the inhalation of smoke and toxic fumes in the early stages of the fire. More detailed analysis showed that among those killed by fires in the home, a high proportion came from vulnerable groups such as people suffering from alcohol or drug-abuse problems, disabled people and elderly people with restricted mobility. It was also clear that the incidence of serious fires leading to death or injury was disproportionately high in certain types of property, such as multi-occupied privately rented houses. None of these figures was new or unfamiliar. They had been widely known within the service for years. Yet they had not proved to be the catalyst for change that might have been expected. The figures spoke for themselves and did not require sophisticated data analysts to point out the huge scope for saving lives through targeted fire prevention work, including the installation of smoke alarms and home fire-safety checks to stop incidents occurring in the first place. Good progress had already been made in reducing the risk of fire caused by flammable materials in new furniture as a result of the Foam Filled Furniture Regulations of the late 1980s, but many people, particularly in poorer neighbourhoods, were still living in homes full of older fixtures and fittings that were not fire-proof and, once ignited, could quickly generate volumes of toxic smoke. To add to the risk, they were more likely to depend on types of heating such as paraffin stoves that could easily cause a fire.

If there was clearly a need to give much greater emphasis to fire prevention, it was also timely to review the nature of the work being undertaken by the Fire Service, for this too had been subject to dramatic changes over the 50 years since the legislation governing the service had been put in place. Responding to road traffic accidents had progressively absorbed an increasing proportion of firefighters' time, which was hardly surprising, given the exponential growth in the number of motor vehicles on the road in the intervening years. The increase in such activity also highlighted new opportunities for saving lives in addition to rescuing people from fires. If the first responder to reach a serious incident such as a road traffic accident (and this was often the Fire Service) was equipped with a defibrillator or other life-saving equipment and the crew were trained in its use, their early intervention could prove critical in saving the lives of people who had been seriously injured. Yet the 1947 Act prevented fire authorities from purchasing equipment specifically for non-firefighting purposes.

There were also new pressures emerging from the much wider use of automated fire alarms in commercial premises and public service buildings. While the presence of such alarms helped to raise awareness of risk and so facilitated early escape by people potentially threatened by fire, the equipment often malfunctioned or was set off accidentally, so an increasing amount of firefighters' time was being taken up in responding to false alarms. This posed a clear challenge to find ways of checking whether or not the alarm was genuine before one or more crews were despatched unnecessarily. Within three months of my taking on the ministerial responsibility for the Fire Service, a further massive challenge was posed by the 9/11 terrorist attacks on New York and Washington. This obviously called into question our preparedness for responding to such incidents, were they to occur in the UK. There was no doubt about the willingness of firefighters to tackle such events. The bravery of the New York firefighters, many of whom lost their lives responding to the attack on the World Trade Center, had earned worldwide admiration, and I was confident that British firefighters would similarly rise to a comparable challenge if it were to happen here. But were they adequately equipped to deal with some of the risks that now were assuming far greater importance? Rescuing people from collapsed buildings often required specialist lifting equipment that was not always readily available. Similarly the threat of chemical attacks, highlighted by the use of sarin gas on the Tokyo underground in 1995, had already posed the question of how the service would be able to respond if there were a requirement for immediate decontamination of victims and firefighters who had been exposed to such a risk. All of this demonstrated the urgent need to review the service's capacity to respond to such threats and to ensure that appropriate new search and rescue and decontamination equipment was procured to facilitate such work.

It was therefore very clear to the fresh eyes looking at the service in DTLR in 2001 that much more needed to be done to promote fire prevention and a wider agenda of public safety and resilience. It seemed obvious that this could lead to very significant reductions in the levels of death and injury caused by fires and other threats to individuals and communities. Even if all of this evidence had not been sufficient to prompt the necessary reforms, other circumstances did. In the way that crises can sometimes paradoxically provide a powerful catalyst for positive change, the looming industrial dispute proved not just a challenge, but also an opportunity. The fact that the reform agenda had not previously been promoted as vigorously as it might have been reflected three main influences. The first was the relatively low status afforded to the Fire Service in both central and local government. There were, in effect, five different types of fire authority in England. In many county areas responsibility lay with a committee of the county council. In other county areas where local government reorganisation had created a patchwork of unitary authorities, combined fire authorities had been formed, representing the various local authorities within that area. In one area where a single unitary authority had been created, it became the fire authority. In metropolitan areas, the responsibility lay with metropolitan fire authorities, again comprising representatives from the different local authorities within the area. Finally, in London a region-wide fire and emergency planning authority (LFEPA) had been created as part of the GLA. In total there were 47 separate authorities, ranging hugely in size and capacity.

Not only was this governance structure unusual, it also failed to deliver the high-calibre oversight that was needed to guide the operation and development of a crucially important public service. Too often, councillors were appointed to serve on fire authorities or fire committees to make up the numbers rather than because they had the skills and commitment to make a difference and to challenge long-established and outdated assumptions or working patterns. This unquestionably had contributed to the failure of the service to recognise the need to adapt to a changed environment, changing demands and newly emerging threats.

It might have been expected that the service's institutions, and in particular the Chief Fire Officers Association (CFOA) and Her Majesty's Inspectorate, would have provided the impetus for change, but neither had acted as an effective voice for reform. While there were impressive individual chief fire officers in particular areas, they did not, unlike their counterparts in the Police Service, enjoy the same degree of statutory operational independence, and they had often encountered real difficulties in taking forward reforming initiatives when seeking approval from their fire authority, on which the FBU often exercised significant influence. This inevitably had a damping effect on the willingness of senior officers to propose changes, for example to the deployment of staff and equipment, that they knew were likely to be controversial or to arouse union opposition. The Inspectorate was widely perceived to be too close to the fire brigades to act as a catalyst for reform. As the independent review (described below) concluded:

> Using the national standards of fire cover as a benchmark for inspection has reinforced the status quo rather than brought about change.[1]

In Whitehall too there had been little appetite to challenge the status quo. The minister responsible for the Fire Service was seen as a relatively low-key appointment, and the service had not featured prominently in the list of public services on which the newly elected Labour government had focused its reform agenda after 1997. In its 2001 manifesto, which was stuffed full of pledges to reform, modernise and improve education, health, local government, policing and other public services, there was simply no reference to fire. No doubt this reflected the political imperative to avoid anything that might prompt a repeat of a divisive industrial dispute as had occurred in the 1970s. Through the following quarter of a century, under governments of different persuasions, ministers and officials had been careful to avoid even discussing, let alone pressing changes that might generate a hostile response from the FBU. The 'benign neglect' had been deliberate, and not simply a product of this being something of a policy backwater. As Philip Wood, the senior official in DTLR and ODPM responsible at the time for the Fire Service, aptly commented, it illustrated the difficulty in dealing with a medium-sized problem – big enough to cause political trouble if confronted, small enough to be ignored without any apparent adverse consequences, at least in the short term.

By throwing down the gauntlet in the form of a claim for a 40% (yes, that was the figure) increase in firefighters' pay, the FBU made it inevitable that the problem would be confronted. It also ensured that wider issues about the way the service operated and how it should respond to the challenges of the early 21st century in the most efficient and cost-effective way would need to be examined in detail. While there had been local disputes affecting individual fire authorities in the intervening period there had been no national dispute since the 1970s, and the dispute that led to the 2002 strike highlighted the inadequacy of the existing institutions to cope with such an eventuality. The National Joint Council (NJC), through which negotiations between the employers and trades unions were conducted, was large and bureaucratic and simply not up to the job. Most of the 47 separate fire authorities understood that the pay claim submitted by the FBU was unrealistic and unaffordable, but few were willing to take a lead in facing down a claim that they had no means of affording. Within the NJC framework, central government had no formal role, even though the cost of any settlement would have had to be met largely from government funding. This clearly unsatisfactory situation called for leadership and a new approach.

The Bain Review[2] was the government's response to the challenge. Sir George Bain, then Vice Chancellor of Queen's University, Belfast was asked to conduct a short but thorough and rigorous independent review of the whole service and the pay claim submitted by the FBU. He was supported by Sir Michael Lyons, former chief executive of Birmingham City Council, and Sir Tony Young, a former president of the Trades Union Congress. Their review was conducted between September and December 2002 and their conclusions were overwhelmingly persuasive. The tone was set in the foreword to their report:

> We did not realise until we started this review just how much potential for reform exists in the current Fire Service. We were surprised at the extent to which the Fire Service has fallen behind best practice in the public and private sector. While there are excellent examples of change and new working practices, regrettably they are not widespread. This has resulted from a combination of factors, including an unsatisfactory industrial relations environment, a weak management system, and a lack of any feeling of ownership by those involved in managing the Service....
>
> The Fire Service needs to be changed from top to bottom and every aspect of its work reformed to bring it into line with best practice at the start of the twenty-first century.... Too many people still die as

a result of fires in the United Kingdom. We do not compare well with other countries, and we have made little or no progress in recent years in driving down the threat of fire and other accidents. While it may be an unachievable aspiration that no-one should die from fire in the future, we believe there is plenty of scope to drive down fatalities, injuries, loss of property and damage to the environment to negligible levels. This requires the combination of a focus on fire prevention rather than incident response, different working practices, and a modern, flexible, risk-based approach to allocating resources....[3]

On the issue of pay they were equally clear that significant increases were not justified on the basis of the existing pay system, but that this too should be radically overhauled and a new, more flexible system introduced linking rewards to improvements in productivity and the development of new skills. The government had already made it very clear to the local authority employers that any pay award not affordable within existing public expenditure parameters had to be met out of demonstrable efficiency savings, for which there was considerable scope.

The Bain Report was a clarion call for reform in a service that had been left in a time warp, approaching its duties and conducting its industrial relations in ways that smacked of the attitudes of a bygone era. It was all the more persuasive coming as it did from three individuals all of whom had impeccable credentials for undertaking their task in a fair-minded and independent way. Sir George Bain was widely respected in trades union circles and had demonstrated his commitment to fairness in the workplace as chairman of the Low Pay Commission, which had overseen the introduction of the National Minimum Wage. His report could not be dismissed as biased or irrelevant, although some in the FBU attempted to treat it that way. It clearly set out a highly challenging agenda for reform and had to be taken very seriously. As the minister responsible for responding to the Bain Report as well as handling the dispute, which was still live, I was acutely conscious of the opportunity it presented to achieve real change that could deliver huge benefits to the public and to firefighters.

However, in the inevitably highly charged atmosphere of a bitter strike, it was unrealistic to expect Bain's admirable blueprint to receive the unanimous support it deserved. The FBU, which had declined the invitation to submit evidence to the Bain Review, was not ready to engage in a constructive dialogue about the future of the service. But in the weeks following the publication of the Bain Report, the strike collapsed. While the public remained sympathetic to firefighters, reflecting admiration for the vital and dangerous service they perform, the size of the union's pay claim and the behaviour of some of its leaders[4] undermined their case, and it was not surprising that they seized the opportunity of talks at Acas (the Advisory, Conciliation and Arbitration Service) in December 2002. The threat of further strike action receded and the industrial action finally came to an end in the early months of 2003. Throughout this tense and difficult period I was struck by the judgement and resolution of both Tony Blair and John Prescott. The Prime Minister rightly concluded that while there was public sympathy for the firefighters, the scale of their claim was so unreasonable that a resolute but fair response from government would prevail. The Deputy Prime Minister, for all his deep connections with the trades unions, knew that in the national interest we had to resist an unjustified pay claim. Their joint commitment to face down the FBU's pay claim but at the same time make full use of the Bain Report as a catalyst for reform was a classic illustration of the effectiveness of the combination of these two different personalities at the very top of government.

In the following months, it was clear to me that we had to move quickly to seize this historic opportunity to reform the service. Some years earlier I had been give very wise advice on the importance of momentum and symbolism in government.[5] Governments acting decisively and with a clear understanding of the goals they need to score can achieve remarkable outcomes. Conversely, a loss of momentum (as occurred with HIPs – see Chapter Five) or the lack of clear objectives (as was apparent in the absence of cross-government support for elected regional assemblies in 2003–04 – see Chapter Seven) can leave governments, even those enjoying large parliamentary majorities, vulnerable to attack from their opponents. In the aftermath of the fire dispute we had to drive forward the reform agenda with determination. So, in spring 2003 we published a White Paper, 'Our Fire and Rescue Service', setting out the government's agenda for reform. The extended title, incorporating the word 'Rescue' as well as 'Fire', was a logical recognition of the wider responsibilities now being undertaken by the service, including rescuing members of the public from a range of hazards in addition to fires. Much of the White Paper was based on the Bain Report's recommendations, but in several areas we were able to flesh out what had of necessity been outline proposals in a report produced to an exceptionally demanding timetable. The White Paper itself was also prepared to a very tight timetable and followed swiftly by new legislation[6] giving effect to the policies spelled out in the White Paper and clearly defining the role that the service was expected to perform, with prevention and a focus on saving lives, not only from fire, very much at the forefront. The input of the civil service team, headed by Alun Evans, was crucial to the successful publication of the White Paper and passage of the Act.

Whereas the framework put in place by the 1947 Act had rested on rigid national standards for the deployment of the service's resources, allowing little local discretion to vary provision in response to changing patterns of need and demand, the 2004 Act required each fire and rescue authority to develop its own locally based Integrated Risk Management Plan. The aim was to ensure local ownership of decisions on the deployment of resources, worked up in response to a detailed assessment of the risks likely to face the local community, and so incentivising local initiative and innovation. The government's role was to change from having been the largely passive custodian of existing standards (no local fire station could be closed without agreement of the Secretary of State) to a new and more strategic role, publishing a national framework setting out expectations and giving guidance on how local fire and rescue authorities might respond but leaving individual authorities responsible for their decisions. An inspection regime, involving the Audit Commission, was put in place to monitor how fire and rescue authorities were responding to the new challenges, using similar methodology to the Comprehensive Performance Assessments of local government (see Chapter Eight), while the Fire Service Inspectorate, which had notionally been responsible for this previously, was to refocus its work on promoting good practice and supporting the service reform programme. At the same time a series of changes were made to the various institutions that supported the work of the service, including winding up the ineffective Central Fire Brigades Advisory Council and reforming the NJC to provide a better basis for negotiating terms and conditions of employment within the service. Responsibility for the service was already devolved to Scotland and Northern Ireland. The Act completed the process by devolving responsibility to Wales too.

The White Paper had been published at the same time as the government's proposals for elected regional assemblies (see Chapter Seven). With the service already managed on a regional basis in London, accountable through the LFEPA to the Greater London Authority, there was an obvious logic in considering the move to a regional structure elsewhere in England, as a number of the service's key challenges, such as dealing with major emergencies, floods or terrorist incidents required cooperation across a wider area than that of most of the smaller authorities. The Bain Report had considered the issue of the number and size of fire authorities in England. The 47 separate authorities in England varied enormously in size, from very large brigades in London, large metropolitan brigades in areas such as the West Midlands and Greater Manchester, to much smaller brigades in predominantly rural areas such as North Yorkshire or the Isle of Wight. Bain highlighted the extent to which some of the new challenges facing the service, such as the 'New Dimension' programme (involving substantial investment in new specialist equipment to allow a more effective response to the threat of terrorist attack, flooding and other major natural disasters), were beyond the capacity of all but the largest brigades. This called, at the least, for effective cross-border cooperation, but also posed the question of whether amalgamation of some of the smaller authorities or the creation of region-wide authorities might be a better long-term solution.

Similar issues arose in respect of the control rooms used to take calls from the public and mobilise fire appliances. Each authority operated its own separate control room, but because the number of incidents varied massively from area to area the cost ranged from £18 per incident in London to £168 per incident in the Isle of Wight. Bain recognised the case for amalgamations to achieve greater efficiency but, rather than recommending any specific new model, proposed that those authorities that decided to keep their own centre should be required to demonstrate to the Audit Commission that this was a cost-effective option. The problem with this approach was that leaving each fire authority to determine how its local control room would operate and the equipment it would use made it difficult to ensure a coherent national network of control centres using compatible technology, and so able to back each other up and ensure effective cross-border mobilisation where necessary.

The conclusion the government reached was that where any region voted for an elected regional assembly, the Fire and Rescue Service should be reconstituted on a regional basis, as in London, and should be accountable to the regional assembly. Elsewhere, fire and rescue authorities would remain responsible for most services within their area but would be required to work together with other authorities within their region through regional management boards on those activities, such as procurement, training, control centres and the New Dimension programme, that needed, for both operational and financial reasons, to be managed across a wider area. As with the New Dimension programme, under which the new urban search and rescue and decontamination equipment had been procured by government, the establishment of regional control centres would be taken forward by government under a project called FireControl. While there was much to commend such an approach, which sought to divide responsibilities logically between national, regional and local bodies, reflecting the different levels at which different aspects of the service's work needs to be discharged, it failed to survive the fall-out from the increasingly bitter political divisions over the government's regional devolution plans as described below.

Another key theme was the need for the service to recruit from a wider pool of talent. For some time concerns had been voiced at the extent to which fire brigades were disproportionately composed of white men. The Bain Report shockingly revealed that at that point in time, and despite many prior calls for a more diverse workforce, 'the service is 98.3% male and 98.5% white'. The report did not pull its punches:

> We have been frankly appalled at some of the stories we have heard of bullying and harassment. The harassment has been both racial and sexual, even given the very small numbers of non-white and female personnel in the service. Such behaviour is illegal as well as being morally repugnant.[7]

With a strong focus now being put on community fire safety work, it was all the more important to put an end to such behaviour and to recruit much more widely from the communities that the service was there to serve. The importance of this was brought home to me very forcibly by an example of a fire safety initiative in Merseyside to reach the Chinese community, which had suffered disproportionately from deaths and injuries caused by preventable fires. The recruitment of staff from within the Chinese community to spearhead this work was, I was told by the Chief Fire Officer, crucial to the success of this initiative. The commitment of the country's senior fire officers and their association, the CFOA, was hugely important to the reform programme. I met regularly with the CFOA both during the dispute and through the subsequent two and a half years to discuss how the service could most effectively recover and move forward with the series of changes set out in the White Paper and legislation. The ability of the various fire authorities to provide a robust and coherent response to the union's pay claim and threatened industrial action had clearly been tested in the course of the dispute and found wanting. Without firm government intervention the outcome could have been very different. It was therefore essential to give clear assurances to both senior fire officers and their authorities that the government would not walk away now that the dispute was over.

So, what came of this complex and multifaceted reform agenda? The answer is mixed. On the one hand, there were very substantial gains from the higher priority accorded to the prevention and community fire safety agenda. The House of Commons Communities and Local Government Select Committee carried out a detailed inquiry in 2005–06 into the impact of the changes introduced following the 2003 White Paper and the 2004 Fire and Rescue Services Act. Its conclusions, set out in a report published in summer 2006, were unequivocal:

> There is little doubt that the emphasis on prevention is promoting fire safety: the numbers both of fires and accidental deaths continue to fall. In the 12 month period up to 30 June 2005 the number of 'primary' fires (that is fires involving property, vehicles and/or casualties) fell by 13 per cent compared with the previous year, with fires in the home falling by 7 per cent. Fire related deaths fell by 16 per cent over the same period while deaths from accidental dwelling fires fell by 21 per cent. The CFOA highlighted this point stating 'In real terms we can claim that at least 78 more people are walking our streets today as a result of our fire safety initiatives.'[8]

Nor was this just a short-term improvement. Seven years later, in a report commissioned by the Coalition government, the then Government Chief Fire and Rescue Adviser, Sir Ken Knight, who had previously been Fire Commissioner for London, emphasised the scale of the advances made over the previous decade:

> The latest half-year statistics published in March 2013 show the continuation of the trend, with total fires from April to September 2012 down 37 per cent on the same period in 2011, and incidents overall down 17 per cent.
>   Over the longer term, the reduction in risk to the public from fire is even more dramatic. In 2011/12, 186 people died in accidental fires in the home. This

is 60 per cent lower than the average figure we saw annually in the 1980s. Firefighters themselves are much safer today, even though they risk their lives to save the public ...

It is clear that the cumulative effect of building and furniture regulations, Integrated Risk Management Planning and the localisation of decision making, and importantly the fire prevention and protection work carried out by fire and rescue authorities has significantly reduced the risk of fire in England.[9]

While the impact of the reforms was clearly hugely positive in terms of outcomes for the public and the reduction of fires, the proposed changes to the institutions and structures of fire authorities made little progress. Only two amalgamations have taken place, bringing together, respectively, the Devon and Somerset and, most recently, the Dorset and Wiltshire fire authorities. Although the experience of the first amalgamation was positive, it took eight years before this example was followed. Yet, as Sir Ken Knight so trenchantly observes in his 2013 report:

No-one setting out to make an efficient model for the delivery of fire and rescue services for England would develop the model we now have; it has largely been driven by, and subordinate to, wider local government changes. It cannot make sense to have the current range of fire and rescue authorities, each with attendant and often different governance structures, spend levels, senior leaders, and organisational and operational quirks.[10]

Ironically, more far-reaching reforms have been implemented in other parts of the United Kingdom, with Scotland opting to combine all its previous separate fire authorities into a single Scottish fire authority. By contrast, England still has 45 separate authorities, almost every one of which continues to operate its own separate control room. The collapse of the FireControl project is the most significant failure in the programme of reforms set out in the 2003 White Paper, and the reasons for this merit further analysis. The logic behind a rationalisation of the arrangements for managing calls to the fire service and mobilising crews and appliances to tackle fires and other emergencies was overwhelming. Local knowledge, which had previously been the main justification for keeping control rooms local, was becoming less and less important with the spread of mobile phones and Geographic Information Systems, which allowed the location of callers to be automatically identified and appliances mobilised and directed to the site of the incident without dependence on a control room operator to guide the crew to the right location. At the same time there were significant savings to be made if the level of cost per call achieved in the largest and most efficient control centres could be matched elsewhere. Even excluding the Isle of Wight outlier, the cost per incident in other smaller authorities (£91 in Northumberland, £82 in Lincolnshire) was several times greater than the £18 per incident cost in London, which had successfully merged its previous three control centres in the early 1990s into one covering the whole region.[11] Additionally, there were the potentially huge benefits from having compatible and networked systems in all authorities, so that each could be backed up by another in the event of technical failure or an exceptionally high volume of calls and the crew and appliance nearest to the incident could be mobilised even if it came from a neighbouring authority area. All of these considerations were given added weight by the threat of serious large-scale incidents, whether caused by natural disaster or by terrorist attack, which would require a coordinated response involving several brigades.

Indeed the consultants Mott MacDonald had recommended in 2000 a reduction in the number of control rooms, initially to 21 and eventually to 9.[12] In an update of this report in 2003 they recommended the immediate establishment of nine control centres – one in each English region – and the government gave a commitment to delivering this through the FireControl project in December 2003. It was anticipated that the new control rooms would be phased in over a six-year timetable, with the programme due to be completed in 2009. In the event, the programme was subject to serious delays and cost over-runs and was cancelled by the incoming Coalition government in 2010.

What had gone wrong? The National Audit Office conducted an investigation, published in July 2011, that pinpointed a number of reasons, of which the failure of the responsible government department (initially ODPM, later DCLG) to secure the support of the key players essential to its success was probably the most crucial.[13] The seeds of this can be found in the situation created by the 2002–03 industrial dispute. Central government had to take the lead because of the weakness of the local authority negotiators when faced with an unaffordable and intransigent pay claim. In the aftermath of the dispute the government had continued to make the running, with the 2003 White Paper and 2004 Fire and Rescue Services Act, in order to carry through the reform agenda and replace the institutions and arrangements that had failed to come up to the challenge. While this was broadly supported by the Chief Fire Officers, several fire authorities were concerned at the loss of some of their powers, and their reservations were fuelled by the FBU, which opposed the move to regional control centres because of the loss of jobs involved. The political conflicts over the government's regional plans, which were opposed by the Conservatives and most county councils and which came to a head with the North East referendum at the same time as the FireControl plans were being developed, poured further fuel on the flames. So, instead of there being a broad consensus in support of a project designed to improve the efficiency, resilience and cost-effectiveness of the service, FireControl became increasingly a centrally imposed project, at best grudgingly accepted and too often openly criticised by those at a local level.

Unlike the position in Hackney, where local leaders were available to drive the improvement programme forward, with government support, as described in Chapter Eight, there was a vacuum at the regional level, with no elected assemblies to take ownership of the new control centres and only lukewarm support, at best, from most of the local authority representatives on the regional management boards. The problem was identified at an early stage. In a health check on the project in October 2004, the Office for Government Commerce (OGC) commented:

> The engagement of the RMBs (Regional
> Management Boards) and FRAs (Fire and Rescue
> Authorities) at the political level is patchy. RMB
> Chairs have formally committed their support
> for the programme in writing to the Responsible
> Minister. However at this stage for some this support
> is conditional.[14]

Similar problems occurred at the national project board. In a memo to the Permanent Secretary at the Department in December 2004, a senior civil servant wrote:

> The LGA [Local Government Association] as senior
> user on the Board behaves more as critical stakeholder
> than as corporate contributor to the project, despite
> the official LGA position of support, and inhibits free
> discussion by ODPM members.[15]

The OGC recommended action to remedy the problems on the national project board, and the recruitment of more staff to enable ODPM officials to engage with and win 'hearts and minds' to bolster support at the regional level. But it clearly did not see the problem as a show-stopper, as its overall conclusion was that 'the project is under control and has made significant progress since Gateway 1'. Sadly, the problems did not get resolved but continued to fester over the following years. Rather than responding by engaging more with local fire and rescue authorities, as well as the chief fire officers and their association, and promoting the advantages of the new control centre arrangements, the department appears to have become increasingly defensive. Its perceived failure to provide accurate and timely information to stakeholders about the progress of the project, and the lack of satisfactory answers to concerns voiced by individual fire and rescue authorities, compounded the problem. The absence of good, close working relations between central government and the local authorities that would ultimately be running the new centres was as damaging to the implementation of FireControl as the absence of close working between the DHSS and the local authorities had been damaging to the introduction of Housing Benefit in 1982–83 (see Chapter Three). It was symptomatic of the problem that the individual fire authorities were never contractually committed to occupying the new regional control centres that ODPM and later DCLG were procuring.

Another problem highlighted by the National Audit Office was government's undue dependence on consultants to oversee the introduction of FireControl. This dependence was made worse by a high turnover of senior staff working on the project in its later stages. Indeed the staff turnover was matched by a parallel turnover of ministers. While I had been minister for a full four years from 2001 to 2005, there were four separate ministers responsible for the Fire and Rescue Service between 2005 and 2009. As we have already seen with HIPs (see Chapter Five), such a turnover can seriously undermine long-term projects that require sustained attention and ministerial guidance. Coinciding as it did with a comparable turnover in senior officials, it cannot have helped to restore confidence to a failing project. The civil service has generally had a poor reputation for managing large procurement projects, and the failure of FireControl certainly reinforces this reputation. Yet, ironically, the other major procurement projects undertaken for the Fire and Rescue Service, such as the New Dimension programme, had been delivered successfully, and have proved their worth on numerous subsequent occasions when the specialist equipment has been essential in helping to cope with serious problems caused by, for example flooding and collapsed buildings.

At the time of the abandonment of the project in 2010, it was cited as another example of the failure of governments to manage large and complex IT contracts. Ironically, this had been one of the concerns I had looked at carefully at the outset in 2003. I was reassured at the time that all the capabilities that the new system was due to provide were already in use, albeit in just a few authorities (I had seen and been impressed by the system operated in Norfolk), and therefore there was no need to develop new and untested IT systems. While this was true, the complexity of linking the new national system into the different operational procedures of 47 different authorities had not been anticipated, and this proved a major difficulty to EADS, the contractor to whom the IT contract was let in 2007. Another issue that had been raised early in the process was the potential benefit of combining different emergency service control rooms (Police, Fire and Ambulance) rather than just combining fire control centres. Local pilots had been initiated in Gloucester and Cleveland, but had not delivered the degree of integration hoped for, and the experience had indicated that the challenges, both technical and cultural, that would need to be overcome to establish a national network of cross-service control centres were likely to be much greater than those facing a network serving just the one service. Indeed the Mott MacDonald report had looked at the option of integrated cross-service control centres, but had rejected it as too high a risk. Maybe it was an idea that had been promoted too soon. For now, 13 years on, there is a renewed interest in bringing together the Police, Fire and Ambulance control room services. Hopefully, this will have a better outcome than FireControl. Looking back on the whole sad saga, I cannot but feel sadness and anger at the waste of public money and the waste of the opportunity to deliver a better and more efficient control room service. FireControl should not have been allowed to fail.

The contrast between the very substantial advances made in reducing the numbers of fires and deaths over the decade since the passing of the 2004 Fire and Rescue Services Act and the failure of the FireControl project helps to illustrate a wider truth about the processes of government and of translating policy into practice. Given the relatively short windows of opportunity available to ministers to make a difference, the prospect of achieving transformational change across a wide canvas is not great. Indeed, implementing individual and sharply focused projects or initiatives is both easier and more likely to deliver a successful outcome than wide-ranging, multifaceted reform programmes seeking to change the culture of organisations. This is not said in a defeatist vein, nor to discourage ambition, but, rather, to emphasise the importance of defining realistic and achievable targets. Aiming higher and falling short is not necessarily a mistake, if the advances clearly outweigh the setbacks, but it inevitably leaves a sense of disappointment. It also highlights the need for continuing pressure to keep the agenda moving forward. So, it was for me a fitting postscript to my period as Fire and Rescue Service Minister that my final campaign as an MP, in 2014–15, was to push a reluctant, and instinctively deregulatory, Coalition government into agreeing the need for new regulations to require the installation of working smoke and carbon monoxide alarms in all privately rented homes. This was unfinished business in that after several years of progress in protecting more homes with working alarms, the momentum had stalled in the second decade of the 21st century, particularly in the private rented sector, where around 15% of all homes remained unprotected. In the view of the CFOA, and most representatives of private landlords, the scope for further advances by voluntary means was almost exhausted. Those landlords wanting to do their best had already complied. Regulation would be required to compel the remainder to do the right thing. The government's own impact assessment estimated that this would save more than 20 lives every year, yet only at the very end of the life of the Parliament, in March 2015, did the government finally accept, under sustained pressure, that this measure was necessary. It came into effect in October 2015.[16]

TEN

The challenge of the Thames Gateway

Anyone who looks closely into the economic and social geography of South-East England cannot fail to be struck by the fundamental imbalance between the characteristics of the area to the west of central London and those of that to the east. The same river Thames is the central feature of both areas, meandering gently towards London from the Cotswolds through Oxford, Henley and Maidenhead, passing Windsor and Runnymede before reaching the borders of London at Hampton Court, and then progressing past Richmond, Kew, Chiswick, Putney, Chelsea and Westminster before arriving at the historic centre of the capital, the City and the Tower of London. Simply reciting the names conjures up an image of affluence, culture and style. By contrast, the journey eastwards from the Tower takes us past Rotherhithe, the Isle of Dogs, Deptford, Canning Town, Woolwich, Dagenham, Erith, Purfleet, Dartford, Tilbury, Gravesend and Canvey Island before reaching the sea at Southend. Almost all of these places have a rich history and fine buildings to admire, but the list of names conjures up an altogether more gritty image than do those to the west. That simply reflects the fact that from the late 17th century, when, symbolically, the monarchy relocated from Greenwich to Hampton Court, to the mid 20th century, the area to the east of central London was progressively built over by heavy manufacturing industry and low-value housing for its workforce, while the area to the west disproportionately attracted upmarket residential investment and associated recreational facilities. Whether this was primarily a reflection of the prevailing westerly winds blowing smoke and industrial emissions downwind, or a combination of that and other influences, the trend continued unabated for almost three centuries.

With the decline, particularly since the end of the Second World War, of most of the traditional heavy industries that had dominated the landscape to the east of the City, the imbalance between the two areas became even sharper, with wealth and higher-quality investment heavily over-represented in West London and along the Thames Valley, while problems of poverty, deprivation and a degraded environment were all too frequently concentrated in the east of London and down the Thames estuary. While it had left a problematic legacy, the closure of much of the heavy industry that had dominated the landscape of East London and much of the estuary provided a real opportunity both to transform the physical environment and to create new and better employment and housing prospects for the people who had worked and lived in the area. It also offered a once-in-a-lifetime opportunity to rebalance the economy of South East England. With the area to the west of London increasingly facing overheating pressure, the scope for easing that pressure through the regeneration of the areas to the east was obvious. Indeed, these areas also held real potential opportunities to contribute to and benefit from the renewed expansion of London.

After four decades of decline, reflecting in part the closure of many older industries but also the planned programme of new and expanded towns accommodating outflow from London, the capital's population had again begun to grow in the late 1980s and 1990s. Expanding financial and business service sectors and a range of creative industries attracted increasing numbers of employees both from within the UK and internationally. Redevelopment of derelict brownfield sites was clearly crucial to the provision of many of the new homes and business premises that would be needed to accommodate this growth, and these sites were disproportionately located in the east of London and along the Thames estuary. However, for such a process to work, transformational change was essential to give confidence to potential investors and residents that East London and the Thames estuary would become as desirable and therefore as profitable a location for their business or their homes as West

London and the Thames Valley. Without such change, the risk was that the East would continue only to attract the same types of relatively low-value developments and unimaginative housing estates as had tended to occupy vacant sites in the preceding two to three decades. The outcome would be a perpetuation of a tarnished image reflecting a lower-quality environment and a less vibrant economy than could be found further west.

Such transformational change required visionary planning and a political commitment to drive through the decisions necessary to make the vision a reality. The Conservative government had in the early 1980s established a development corporation in the Docklands area, where substantial acres of formerly industrial land had become available for redevelopment as the docks had closed. Unlike many of my Labour Party colleagues, I had supported this designation, as it seemed the only realistic way to secure the transformational change necessary in the area. It was bitterly opposed by the local authorities, but they had demonstrated neither the will nor the capacity to drive through the far-reaching changes that would be essential if the area was to take on a new lease of life. Simply clinging on to the vestiges of its former industrial character and culture was not likely to secure effective regeneration.

This is not to say that the process of change was not fraught with difficulties. The contrast in the early 1990s between the shining new towers that were beginning to rise from the former derelict docks in Canary Wharf and the continuing deprivation in many of the surrounding areas was a stark one and prompted some challenging reactions, including the election of a British National Party candidate to the Tower Hamlets council in the Millwall ward in 1993. Concern that the top-down imposition of development corporations, focusing mainly on commercial development and the provision of expensive loft apartments for high earners, would ride roughshod over the interests of existing communities was unquestionably a key factor. It led most of the councils in the surrounding areas along the river to the east to reject proposals to extend the London Docklands Development Corporation (LDDC) remit. There was nevertheless a clear need for a new planning framework to guide the redevelopment of those areas. While individual councils had plans for specific locations within their boundaries (my Borough of Greenwich had published interesting proposals for the regeneration of derelict former industrial sites along the waterfront), there were real risks that these would not add up to more than the sum of the parts, when what was needed was a coordinated transformation of the whole of the East Thames Corridor, as the area was initially designated.

The size and geography of the area, stretching from the edge of central London to the estuary, and embracing substantial parts of East London, North Kent and South Essex, posed particular challenges. Although Michael Heseltine, returning to the post of Secretary of State for the Environment in the Major government, was known to favour the extension of the remit of the LDDC, the scale of the East Thames Corridor area made the possibility of a single overarching development corporation impracticable. It would have embraced not just dozens of different local authority areas, but also three separate government regions (London, the South East and the East of England). These considerations led the government to favour the development of a new sub-regional planning framework for the East Thames Corridor. The concept had emerged from the work of SERPLAN, the standing conference of planners from local authorities in London and South East England, and was championed by the doyen of British planners, Professor Sir Peter Hall, who convinced Michael Heseltine that it held the key to a successful transformation of the area east of Docklands. Decades earlier Hall had been instrumental in identifying the opportunity for a corridor of development eastwards from London to the estuary.[1] At the time, planning policy still envisaged an outflow of both population and jobs from London, in line with the thinking of the war-time Abercrombie Report[2] and the post-war New Towns programme. These which had envisaged a ring of new settlements around London (and other cities in Britain) to allow for slum clearance and rebuilding at lower densities than had prevailed in the rapid expansion of 19th-century London. Peter Hall highlighted the importance of transport links to ensure the success and viability of new developments, and presciently promoted the concept of transport-related corridors as against a further ring of freestanding new settlements. Such corridors already existed or were developing on the other sides of London. To the south, one followed the rail line and A23 via Redhill, Gatwick, Crawley and Haywards Heath to Brighton. To the south-west and west there were two corridors, respectively following the A3 and M3 via Guildford and Basingstoke to Southampton and Portsmouth, and the M4 and Great Western Railway line via Reading to Swindon. To the north there were again two corridors, one following the M1 and West Coast Mainline via Milton Keynes and Northampton, the other following the A1 and East Coast Mainline via Stevenage to Peterborough.

Hall's vision of a new linear development to the east of London and along the estuary provided the missing link in the jigsaw and offered an ideal framework for a transformation of the economic geography of South East England. Not only did this hold out prospects for deprived communities in East London and further down the river of attracting new investment and development opportunities; it also offered to the more affluent areas to the west of London the possibility of relieving development pressures in their areas. It is probably because of this coalescence of interests that the East Thames Corridor proposal received such widespread support. Endorsed by Michael Heseltine in 1990, the concept was further developed by consultants Llewellyn-Davies[3] in a 1993 study of the capacity and potential for development in the corridor, and led on to the publication in 1995 of sub-regional planning guidance for the area (RPG9A).[4] In 1995, perhaps reflecting the growing political attention to presentation, the area was renamed the Thames Gateway by David Curry, then the minister responsible for housing and planning, a title that was thought to be more attractive to potential investors and residents.

While the name 'corridor' may have been dropped, it remained the case that transport links (or corridors) were critical to the success of the development plans, as Peter Hall had stressed from the outset. Many of the development sites with the greatest potential to the east of London were difficult to access, and the area as a whole was perceived to be poorly connected. Remedying these disadvantages would clearly be vital if the potential of the Thames Gateway were to be fully realised. At the time that Michael Heseltine gave the initial commitment to the East Thames Corridor the critical transport concern was the Channel Tunnel Rail Link (CTRL). Mainly because of Margaret Thatcher's aversion to public investment in railways, the Channel Tunnel had been constructed with no provision for a high-speed link to London and the rest of the UK. By contrast, the French government had ensured that trains emerging from the tunnel near Calais were immediately linked into its high-speed rail network, facilitating fast access to Lille as well as Paris. But the northern portal of the Tunnel, near Folkestone, linked only into the existing, congested rail lines through Kent and South London into Waterloo. This allowed French President Mitterand to quip at the opening of the Tunnel about Britain's arrangements enabling passengers to admire the beauties of the English landscape as they meandered gently on their way to London. It was a perfect response to the discomfort he must have felt at the choice of London terminus, named after his country's most celebrated military defeat. But, joking apart, that link was clearly a hopelessly inappropriate response to the need for fast international connections, and British Rail was soon looking at alternative routes through Kent and South London for a new high-speed link. Its leaked route plans predictably provoked outrage across all the areas affected, and even when it had changed the alignment to follow the M20, and provided for a lengthy tunnel on the approach to London, the route continued to arouse heated opposition.

The critical change came with the intervention of engineers Arup with an alternative proposal to take the high-speed rail line into Kings Cross (later moved to St Pancras) station instead of Waterloo, via areas along the Thames to the east of London that were crying out for development.[5] Not only did this remove the threat of unwelcome railway engineering works from many of the most hostile areas in Kent and South London, it also opened up potentially huge regeneration opportunities along the route. Strong cases were advanced by interested local authorities and landowners for intermediate stations to facilitate regeneration, with Stratford, promoted by Newham Council, and Ebbsfleet, where the closure of the Blue Circle cement works created a huge development opportunity backed by Dartford, Gravesham and Kent County Council, winning at the expense of Rainham.

The rail line promoters were initially unwilling to agree any intermediate stops, but eventually had to settle for two. The reluctance of transport planners to support new stations on high-speed and other new rail routes is one of the more curious features of recent rail planning in England (it has been seen again in the debates over HS2, and reflects the priority transport planners accord to journey speed rather than wider community and economic benefits) and could, if left unchallenged, as we will see, have had a very damaging impact on the scope for regeneration in East London. In the case of the CTRL, the successful outcome depended on the intervention of Michael Heseltine, who successfully argued the case for the easterly approach route to London, proposed by Arup, with its huge potential regeneration benefits along the East Thames Corridor, against British Rail's preference for the South London route and Treasury opposition to the whole scheme on cost grounds. Ten years later, London's ultimately successful bid for the 2012 Olympic and Paralympic Games depended crucially on the availability of fast rail access to Stratford, which would not have been available had either the British Rail transport planners or the Treasury won the argument.

However, while the CTRL decision was a step forward for the future of the Thames Gateway, too many other transport plans either failed to recognise or perversely rejected opportunities to enable regeneration and development. As MP for Greenwich (from 1992 to 1997) and for Greenwich and Woolwich (from 1997 to 2015) I saw at first hand how a lack of integrated policy making jeopardised the prospects of successful transformation of several major development sites in this one part of the Gateway area. My first insight into the difficulties of securing commitments to necessary transport infrastructure came before I was elected in 1992, when the then preferred route for the proposed Jubilee Underground line extension went north of the river Thames from Canary Wharf to Stratford without any connection to the Greenwich Peninsula immediately to the east. The peninsula, originally marshland surrounded on three sides by a hairpin bend in the river, had in the 19th century become the site of what for a time was the largest gasworks in Europe and had played a significant role in Britain's industrial development. By the late

20th century almost all the industry had closed and huge swathes of land were derelict and abandoned. A curiosity that I discovered when getting to know the far reaches of my constituency was a site near the tip of the peninsula used by Reuters, the news agency, as a base for small hovercraft to transport its employees across the Thames. The rationale for this bizarre transport service was, interestingly, the very one that prompted the campaign for an underground station at North Greenwich, namely the very poor transport links to the peninsula. Surrounded on three sides by the river, the peninsula was accessible from the north only by the Blackwall Tunnel, which was frequently blocked or congested. Frustrated by the long delays experienced by their staff coming from south of the river to their new office on the north bank, near to Canary Wharf, Reuters had set up its own hovercraft service to provide quicker access. This made it all the more extraordinary that those responsible for planning the Jubilee Line extension had not recognised the benefits of taking the tube from Canary Wharf via North Greenwich to Canning Town and Stratford.

Fortunately common sense eventually prevailed, following a vigorous campaign in which British Gas, the principal landowner on the peninsula, Greenwich Council, under the purposeful leadership of Len Duvall, and I pressed the government to reconsider the route and incorporate a station at North Greenwich. Steven Norris, then a minister in the Department for Transport, was both receptive and helpful, and with his support we secured the positive outcome needed to unlock development on the peninsula. As a result, the regeneration of the peninsula has been able to proceed. It is now home to Greenwich Millennium Village (see Chapter Four), the O2 Arena, the world's most successful music venue, and Ravensbourne College, a renowned centre for digital media studies, and has the capacity for 15,000 more homes. The station at North Greenwich, which prior to 1997 stood on a totally derelict site, is now served by eight different bus routes. Such is the volume of users that the Jubilee Line has already had to be upgraded twice to cope with the demand and is currently once again near capacity. It would be nice to think that lessons were learned from the successful outcome of this story, but astonishingly I found myself twice again in the following years having to launch campaigns to reverse foolish short-term decisions against transport enhancements that had huge and obvious regeneration benefits. The first was the station at Cutty Sark, Greenwich on the extension of the Docklands Light Railway (DLR) to Lewisham. The station today is intensively used, situated at the edge of a World Heritage site containing some of London's most iconic historic buildings and tourist attractions. Difficult as it is to understand today, the planners responsible for the DLR extension, prompted mainly by a desire to cut costs – because the transport benefits were obvious – actually took a decision in the mid-1990s to drop this station from the scheme. It took a further forceful public campaign and a substantial financial contribution from Greenwich Council to secure a reconsideration.

Less than 10 years on from that near miss, the whole saga was repeated in spades over the decision by the Department for Transport to drop the planned station at Woolwich from the Crossrail scheme. Crossrail had its origins in the 1980s as a means of increasing East–West transport capacity in central London, with the main section running underground from Paddington to Liverpool Street. It was in part modelled on the Paris RER service, offering larger carriages and therefore greater capacity than the traditional London Underground, but replicating the benefits of frequent stops on Underground and Metro services. At that stage, no extension to Canary Wharf was envisaged, even though the LDDC was already well into its work transforming Docklands. The scheme failed to get approval, partly because of in-fighting within the Conservative parliamentary ranks during John Major's troubled government.

Following Labour's 1997 victory, John Prescott took over responsibility for transport as well as regeneration and housing in the expanded DETR. One of his early challenges was to put High Speed One (as the CTRL is now known) back on track after its private promoters had faced financial difficulties. This required a phasing of the scheme, but ensured its successful completion. Prescott also resurrected the Crossrail scheme, commissioning a study into its potential contribution to East–West connections in London. This study, which was completed in 2002, recommended an extension of the line beyond Liverpool Street to serve Canary

Wharf, and reaching South of the river to Woolwich and Abbey Wood, while another branch proceeded north of the Thames to Stratford and on to Brentford and Shenfield in Essex. Both of these links offered very considerable potential for stimulating and supporting regeneration in East London and the Thames Gateway. The southern route in particular made possible the further development of Canary Wharf, where the new capacity provided by the Jubilee Line had already been largely absorbed. It also offered a real boost to Woolwich, where the economy was still seriously depressed following the closure of the heavy industry that had provided the town's main economic bedrock in the 19th and early 20th centuries.

By the time that the East–West study was complete, however, responsibility for transport had transferred from the DETR and its successor DTLR to a separate Department for Transport, which displayed little or no understanding of the critical role that well-planned transport links can play in supporting regeneration and development. Pressed by the Treasury to limit expenditure on Crossrail, the Department for Transport chose to drop the Woolwich station from the scheme on the grounds that this would save upwards of £300 million. The high cost reflected not just the size of station required for the larger and longer trains envisaged on Crossrail, but mainly its underground location. This was unavoidable, as trains had to cross under the Thames to reach Woolwich and remain underground to pass beneath the Southern Outfall Sewer (part of Sir Joseph Bazalgette's Victorian engineering triumph) immediately to the east of Woolwich.

While, as we were later able to demonstrate, savings could be made through reducing the depth of the station and other engineering changes, all Crossrail underground stations carry a very significant price tag. It was, however, very disappointing to know that a Labour government had, when looking for savings, chosen to sacrifice the station at Woolwich in one of London's poorer neighbourhoods, while still continuing with the planned stations at Bond Street, Tottenham Court Road and Farringdon. Equally disappointing was the reluctance of the mayor and TfL to speak up for Woolwich. My discomfort only grew as I realised through questioning those responsible for the decision, including ministerial colleagues, that regeneration benefits were largely disregarded in the benefit/cost analysis used to evaluate the economic impact of Crossrail. The Department for Transport appeared interested only in transport and passenger benefits, and the Treasury too was, bizarrely, indifferent to the potential for regeneration. While there were, as we were later able to prove with the support of the transport planners working for Crossrail, significant transport gains from a station at Woolwich, there was just as powerful a case for a Woolwich station in the impact that it would have in attracting investment to the town and supporting new homes and wider regeneration across the surrounding area.

As I left government in the spring of 2005, I determined to use the freedom of the back benches to launch a campaign to reverse the decision to drop the Woolwich station. Fortunately my experience of the Channel Tunnel scheme almost 20 years earlier proved very useful when considering how best to secure the right outcome. In recent years major rail schemes in England have been approved by Parliament using the hybrid Bill procedure rather than going through the planning process. This curious and in some ways anomalous procedure dates back to the early days of rail in the 19th century, when approval of new railway lines and the location of stations were matters of particular importance to many landowners and industrialists, who sought to use their parliamentary influence to secure favourable outcomes. Having served on the Channel Tunnel Bill Committee in 1986–87, I was well aware of the potential opportunity of a hybrid Bill committee to secure significant changes in rail schemes subject to legislation. So, having failed to convince my colleagues in government through gentle persuasion, I advised Greenwich Council to use the option of petitioning the committee charged with considering the Crossrail scheme, and set about presenting the most powerful possible case to them.

Psychology played a significant role in the process. Few MPs choose to serve on a hybrid Bill committee. It takes up a disproportionate amount of time, often lasting for a year or more, during which time members of the committee are seriously constrained from active engagement in other parliamentary work. In my case, I had volunteered for the Channel Tunnel Bill Committee as a newly elected MP because I was interested in the subject, but as the months passed I realised just how time consuming a commitment it was. With the Crossrail Bill, most of the members had been nominated for the committee by their whips as a punishment for voting against the party line in other parliamentary debates.[6] For them, the one potential compensation for their many hours of service on the committee would be the opportunity to secure a significant change in the Bill that would not otherwise have happened. I made it my task to persuade as many of the committee members as possible that the Woolwich station provided just such an opportunity to make their mark.

The committee was convinced by the case, and in late summer 2006 submitted a report recommending that the Bill be amended to include the Woolwich station. As well as preparing evidence supporting the case for the station, I had been exploring with our advisers ways to reduce the cost so as to make it easier for the government to concede. I have already referred to various design and engineering changes adopted to reduce cost. At the same time we began discussions with Berkeley Homes, which was already undertaking a major housing development in the former Royal Arsenal at Woolwich. As this was the site previously identified as the most appropriate location for the Woolwich station there was obvious potential to seek a developer contribution to the station, which would, if built, enhance the attractiveness and value of the development. Tony Pidgley, chairman of the Berkeley Group, was up for a deal and agreed to meet the costs of constructing the station box, which would also serve as foundation for the housing he proposed to build over the station. In return Greenwich Council agreed a revision to the planning consent to increase the housing numbers on site.

In most circumstances this should have been more than sufficient to sweeten the necessary U-turn by government, but the government was still not prepared to accept reason. Instead, the Secretary of State, Douglas Alexander, refused the committee's recommendation and tried to suggest that it had been exceeding its powers, a claim that we had little difficulty in debunking.[7] The claim was all the more curious coming from the Secretary of State for Transport, because the Crossrail team had declined to give evidence to the committee against the Woolwich station in the light of its obvious transport benefits.

It later became clear that Alexander was being pressured by the Treasury not to concede. One of Gordon Brown's Special Advisers, Shriti (later Baroness) Vadera, appears to have taken it upon herself to tell Alexander that it was a trial of strength that he had to win. He could not have received worse advice. The committee, incensed at the high-handed rejection of its recommendation, raised the stakes. Its chairman, Alan (now Sir Alan) Meale, whom I also knew well as a former minister in DETR, was particularly angered by the dismissive response to the soundly based recommendation and privately warned the government that if it did not adopt a more reasonable approach he would adjourn the committee indefinitely. This would leave the government with no way of progressing the Bill, and therefore the whole Crossrail scheme would be left in limbo. This, finally, did the trick, and through tortuous negotiations over the winter 2006–07 an agreement was reached under which the Crossrail Bill was amended to include the Woolwich station, while Berkeley Homes committed to build the station box and to contribute to its fitting-out, together with contributions from the other key stakeholders, including Greenwich Council and the GLA. The government put the best interpretation on the deal, claiming that this meant that there would be no additional government expenditure on the station, which left unanswered the awkward question of why it felt it appropriate to meet the cost of constructing a station at Bond Street but not at Woolwich. Never mind. The outcome was a triumph for common sense and already, even before the station opens in 2018, has given a huge stimulus to the regeneration of Woolwich.

The Woolwich station story is symptomatic of a wider problem across the Thames Gateway. For an area that is known to suffer from poor connectivity, the absence of well-integrated planning of transport and other infrastructure to support the transformation of the Gateway is clearly a serious weakness. There are, sadly, loads of other illustrations in addition to those I have described in this chapter. The long drawn-out saga of failure to build river crossings from Becton to Thamesmead to improve cross-river access between two relatively disadvantaged and under-developed areas, and from Silvertown to Greenwich to relieve the still hopelessly congested Blackwall Tunnel, are obvious examples. Hopefully, a resolution enabling these long-overdue crossings to be built will be confirmed before long, but the protracted delay in giving effect to such vital infrastructure needs is indicative of the failure to ensure a properly joined-up approach to planning investment in the Thames Gateway.

Of course the transport issue with the greatest potential impact on the estuary was the location of London's hub airport. In the early 1970s, following rejection by the Heath government of the Roskill Commission's recommendation to build London's new hub airport at Cublington in Buckinghamshire, work briefly began on Maplin Sands, north-east of Southend. The logic for an estuary location for London's premier airport was powerful. Unlike Heathrow, the estuary site could be approached in the prevailing westerly direction without the associated noise and potential safety risks of overflying densely populated areas of London. Again, in contrast to Heathrow, there was scope for further expansion without having to demolish substantial numbers of homes, and without adding to the overheating pressures on the West London economy and the serious air-quality issues around Heathrow.

An airport located in the estuary would also have given huge and early impetus to the rebalancing of the economy of South East England and the regeneration of the whole Thames Gateway area. Of course the creation of a new hub airport location would require very substantial infrastructure investment to enable passengers to travel quickly, and mainly by train, to and from London, Europe and the North. But location in the estuary would have allowed quick connections to High Speed 1, and a new rail connection from the airport to a North London terminus would also have made possible direct links from the Midlands and the North. This logic led to the resurrection of the concept (which had been abandoned in the economic crisis in the mid-1970s) in the early 2000s as pressures mounted for further expansion of airport capacity. But, despite forceful advocacy from the mayor of London, Boris Johnson, and a small group of parliamentary supporters, myself included, it did not gain sufficient traction to win support from either government or the Airport Commission, which ended up making sub-optimal and hugely problematic proposals for an additional runway at Heathrow.

Transport and other infrastructure planning failures are not, however, alone in explaining under-performance in the Thames Gateway. Nor is transport investment a complete panacea, as the delay of almost 20 years in bringing forward development plans at Ebbsfleet demonstrates. Indeed the failures are a symptom of a wider problem. This has been the absence of an effective overarching delivery agency to ensure that the disparate elements that needed to be in place were properly planned and coordinated. As I have already said, the area was too large to be overseen by a single development corporation, and such a body would almost certainly have encountered fierce opposition from the many local authorities whose powers, particularly in respect of planning and land assembly, would have been taken from them by such a corporation. However, the harsh reality is that the two parts of the Gateway that have seen truly transformational change are the two that have benefited from powerful development agencies, the LDDC on the Isle of Dogs and the Olympic Delivery Authority (ODA) in Stratford.

Both areas were transformed by powerful, single-purpose bodies with a clear remit and, in the case of the ODA, a tight and inflexible timetable. Their success is evidenced not just by the very visible redevelopment on the ground, but also by their impact in driving a wider change in the public perception of the area. There has been a perceptible shift in London's centre of gravity in the early 21st century, as part of which the Isle of Dogs and Stratford are no longer seen as relatively remote and run-down locations somewhere to the east of London. Instead, they are attracting ever more investment as magnets for large and prestigious businesses, for cutting-edge and creative industries and for substantial new residential developments. To this extent, the original ambition for the East Thames Corridor, transforming its image and the economic, social and environmental quality of the area, is being achieved.

Travel further to the east, however, through outer London and along the estuary, and the picture is much patchier. There certainly have been successes. Each local authority area along the river is able to highlight examples of new residential, leisure and commercial developments. However, these tend to be isolated beacons in an area still characterised by too many derelict and undeveloped sites. There is nowhere near the same sense of transformation as at Canary Wharf or Stratford. Indeed, the further east one travels the greater the uncertainty one feels as to whether and, if so, when the promised transformation will happen. Of course the LDDC and the ODA both were able to deploy substantial resources that were not available on the same scale elsewhere, but it is not the case that the rest of the Gateway was denied funding opportunities. A strategic partnership was established in the early 21st century to oversee the Thames Gateway, with access to significant spending power, and it did support a variety of different initiatives throughout the Gateway. There were also urban development corporations set up to facilitate regeneration and development in Thurrock and East London. However, the sum of their work has not resulted in the wider transformational change that was originally hoped for, and has left a real sense of a job only partly done. In truth the strategic partnership never got an effective grip on the implementation of the strategy and failed to drive forward the key inputs that could have secured faster and more substantial progress. The Thames Gateway remains an area of opportunity, but it is a patchwork, still characterised as much by the relics of its industrial past as by the harbingers of a Brave New World. The bigger vision has been lost; in its place we are left with a series of fragmented local initiatives that do not add up to more than the sum of the parts. We are a long way from the scenario that inspired the East Thames Corridor concept, in which investors would flock as enthusiastically to Erith, Purfleet, Tilbury or Sheerness as they would to Chiswick, Richmond or Maidenhead.

ELEVEN

Conclusions

Over the more than 40 years in which I have been involved in political activity, some of which has been described in the preceding chapters, I have inevitably met and worked with a very large number of people. Some were obviously better endowed with skills, energy, intelligence and imagination than others, and some applied themselves with far greater determination than others to achieving results. But there were very few who did not want to do a good job and to leave a positive mark on their community, their city, their country or the world.

The overwhelming majority of people who get involved in politics do so in, my experience, because they want to make a positive difference. They have their own view as to how best to do so, and in some cases their views are diametrically opposed to those of others. That is the nature of politics. But I could count on the fingers of one hand the number of people I have known who appear to have got themselves involved in the political process in the UK with no aspiration to change things for the better. They may well have had other motives, and, not surprisingly, personal ambition featured strongly among these; but in almost every case these motives were combined with and, in many cases subordinate to, a commitment to public service and a passionate belief that their input could make other people's lives better. Yet surprisingly few end their careers or their period of political engagement feeling satisfied that they have delivered what they had hoped to achieve. This in part reflects the cyclical nature of political ups and downs. The swing of the electoral pendulum ends many political careers sooner than expected or intended. Being in the wrong place at the wrong time, or being a member of a political party at a time when its fortunes are on the wane, can be a devastating blow to hopes and ambition.

But even among those who have had the good fortune to hold office for a period of years there are too many who feel frustrated that they were not able to make the most of those opportunities. While the much-quoted Enoch Powell aphorism 'all political careers end in failure' is neither true nor helpful in distinguishing the degrees of success or failure that apply in most cases, it does nevertheless convey the bleak pessimism that characterised his career and all too commonly affects others involved in the political process. Too often that pessimism leads to a blame culture where the individual seeks to explain his or her failure to achieve more by reference to the failure of others to do what they should have done. It has been a common theme throughout my lifetime for politicians, of all parties, to blame civil servants for not implementing their policies properly. This complaint is most frequently voiced by those who have a simplistic view of government, in which they believe the key challenge is to take hold of the levers of power on the assumption that if they pull them in the right direction, the desired outcome will be delivered. When this fails to occur, how much easier to blame the civil servants for not seeing that the minister's instructions were put into practice, rather than to question whether there were more fundamental problems or obstacles.

In most other walks of life it is clearly understood that the processes involved in delivering a product or service are complex and multifaceted, and success depends on ensuring that all, or certainly the large majority, of those factors are working to near-optimum efficiency and pulling together in the right direction. It would be unthinkable for a newly appointed managing director of a division of a major manufacturing company to come into post, make a few speeches, brief a few journalists, publish a prospectus for a new product and then sit back, expecting to see the orders rolling in and with the expectation that the company's production capacity would expand dramatically, without any supply or quality-control problems, in response to the surge in demand. Yet that, in broad terms, is what those of the 'take hold of the levers of power' school of political thought believe should happen. It is hardly surprising if they end up disappointed and frustrated.

Reality is very different. Making things happen normally requires a whole series of decisions and actions, including a clear definition of objectives, rigorous testing of all the assumptions underlying the project, meticulous planning, thorough briefing of all the parties involved in the implementation plan, anticipation of potential obstacles, contingency planning to cover unexpected difficulties, reliable mechanisms for monitoring progress against agreed milestones and the capacity to take corrective action when developments are not going entirely according to plan. By contrast, the way in which too many political initiatives are evolved fails on almost all counts. It would be a cruel but not entirely inaccurate caricature to describe the evolution of a typical political policy as progressing from a bright idea dreamed up in a think-tank, to adoption (with only a cursory interrogation of its authors) by a small group of politicians and their advisers who are prompted by a desire to secure political advantage, and so on to evaluation by people with no technical understanding of the subject area, before being inserted hastily into a manifesto with a view to gaining favourable media coverage, and then being trumpeted (assuming electoral success) as almost 'holy writ' because of its status as a manifesto commitment.

The above scenario may, like the fabled TV series *Yes, Minister*, exaggerate the foibles of Whitehall, but it isn't that far from everyday reality. Indeed the evolution of the Conservative government's policy for extending the Right to Buy to tenants of housing associations followed very closely the scenario painted above. And it doesn't end there. The implementation phase of a new policy can be equally dysfunctional, often starting with the policy's being entrusted to a minister who may have had little part in the development of the idea and no previous experience of the subject. He or she will therefore have little understanding of the potential obstacles to successful implementation, and may not know any of the bodies within government and in the wider world whose involvement will be crucial to success. It will then pass through legislative scrutiny, which is designed to show up weaknesses in the scheme but too often fails to do so because of party political pressures to secure the speedy passage of the legislation. Even so, the arcane procedures of the two Houses of the British Parliament usually involve the best part of a year passing before the Bill receives royal assent, during the bulk of which time the minister will be heavily involved in a variety of different tasks. So, he or she will not have had the time and space to give detailed consideration to the processes involved in moving from legislating to implementing the measure. Assuming that the minister is diligent, he or she will probably ask from time to time for progress reports, but will be given reassuring responses from civil servants who will probably be working away desperately behind the scenes to try to make sense of the whole process. The last thing that they will want is any further ministerial instructions, and so they will be wary of giving the minister bad news. It is hardly surprising if things don't always go as well as expected. The best that the unfortunate minister can hope for is a move in the following year's reshuffle to another department with no involvement in the implementation of his former policy. That way, at least, he or she may escape criticism when things unravel.

It does not require the whole chapter of accidents to occur for a policy to fail. A mishap in just one stage of the process may be fatal. Even when a much more rigorous and thorough process has been followed in developing and trialling a policy, as for example with 'sellers' packs' (see Chapter Five), the outcome may still be disastrous because of failings in the implementation process. Given the potential for mishaps along the route, it is surprising that more attention is not focused on how government and Parliament could 'sharpen up their act' to make it more likely that they deliver good government – the very reason for which they exist. Indeed, if this is achieved the outcome is likely to be more job satisfaction for those involved in the political process, with less time wasted on fruitless or doomed activity and more prospect of leaving a positive mark. So, in this concluding chapter I set out a series of proposed reforms to tackle and overcome some of the problems highlighted in earlier chapters, the purpose of which is to make it more likely that policy initiatives can be successfully implemented.

The starting point has to be recognition that government in Britain, and particularly in England, is over-centralised. Two fundamental problems flow from this. First, good government at a sub-national level, whether we are talking about regional, sub-regional, local or neighbourhood, has been and still is inhibited by the absence of powers and opportunities that would attract talented people to get involved in and contribute to the improvement of their area. This is not to say that there are not able players in sub-national tiers of government in England. There are. But sit down and talk to them about their experience, and invariably they will refer to the stifling restrictions on the scope for initiative at their level without the consent of central government. There is a 'chicken and egg' dimension to this. Government ministers and senior civil servants often complain about the weaknesses of local government, arguing that they cannot safely delegate more powers unless they are satisfied that the calibre of local councillors is higher. It was in part to respond to such attitudes that I enthusiastically pursued the local government improvement agenda described in Chapter Eight. But of course the prospect of attracting an on-going supply of able candidates is seriously prejudiced by the absence of powers and opportunities to make a difference. The only way to unravel this conundrum is by 'sucking and seeing' what happens when more powers are devolved. This is not an argument for government washing its hands of any responsibility. It is perfectly reasonable for government to want to monitor progress and take action if things go seriously wrong. The intervention powers are there as described in Chapter Eight. But there must be an opportunity for sub-national tiers of government to assume greater responsibility for determining the future well-being of their areas.

The second fundamental problem that flows from the current over-centralised framework is the overload it places on ministers and civil servants to keep on top of the huge volume of policy for which they are currently responsible. Only a proportion of this is of truly strategic importance that really should receive the close attention of ministers. Much is detail with little or no significance to the government's priorities. Yet, when trying in the early 2000s to persuade colleagues in other government departments to reduce the number of reporting obligations imposed on local authorities I often came up against ferocious resistance. I well remember one such discussion with a colleague who adamantly insisted that to do his job properly he had to receive regular returns on the number of miles of footpath in every local authority in the country! Micro-management on this scale is damaging both to local initiative and to the capacity of ministers to concentrate on truly important strategic issues. The consequence is that we have many more ministers than in the past, and indeed many more than we really need. In turn they spend a disproportionate amount of their time in Whitehall rather than getting around the country, meeting and getting to know the key players in the sectors of the economy or the public services for which they are responsible. Such contacts were, in my experience, vital to understanding the sectors for which I carried responsibility and to building confidence in and support for the various initiatives I was taking. Yet too often the pressures on the ministerial diary inhibit the level of contact that ministers need and should have with the people most directly affected by their decisions, particularly when they are at a distance from London. A programme for devolution of decision making to sub-national tiers of government would therefore free up time and opportunity to help ministers do their job better.

A successful devolution programme should not just involve giving more power to one level of sub-national government. As I have tried to identify in preceding chapters, different responsibilities are best discharged at different levels. When the GLA was established (see Chapter Six) it was given a clearly strategic remit to cover issues that needed to be handled at a city-wide or regional level. These were defined distinctly from local service-delivery issues, which remained the responsibility of the London boroughs. Despite the failure of the proposed introduction of elected regional assemblies (see Chapter Seven), I remain convinced that there is a need for a distinction between local and strategic decision making. The emergence of combined and city-regional authorities, following the Manchester lead, is a step in the right direction, but leaves unanswered the difficult question of how to ensure that some areas are not left out simply because of the inability of the existing authorities in their area to agree a framework for cooperation. There is also a real risk of sub-optimal partnerships and combined authorities being formed not because they represent a logical solution to regional or sub-regional needs but simply because they pose the least threat to existing vested interests. It is also the case that in an already very unequal country, in which London continues to power ahead while many other parts of the country struggle, we really do need to ensure that other regions have powerful voices to argue their corner and match the influence of the London mayor.

At a local level there is also unfinished business. The various moves under different governments since 1990 towards establishing more unitary local authorities have all achieved less than was originally hoped. As a consequence we currently have a curious patchwork quilt of different types of authority in different areas. This is neither logical nor sustainable. A number of the smaller district councils are increasingly challenged by capacity constraints. The argument for the retention of districts always centred on the degree to which they are more local, and so closer to the electorate than the larger counties. However, with increasing focus on some activity being conducted at a parish or neighbourhood level, it would seem sensible to move towards a framework of wholly unitary local authorities in all parts of the country. This would certainly assist the case for devolving more powers both to local authority level and to neighbourhoods – the 'double devolution' agenda that attracted a certain degree of support in the 2005–10 Parliament.[1]

We also need to understand that for certain tasks, and particularly for major development initiatives, special purpose vehicles are probably the best option for securing effective implementation. The lessons of the Thames Gateway (see Chapter Ten) are clearly apposite. Because such bodies have traditionally been seen as a threat to local authorities, it may seem odd that I should be advocating their use at the same time as calling for more devolution of powers from the centre. But although local authorities have traditionally opposed the imposition of such bodies, the two are not inherently in conflict. Development corporations or other special purpose vehicles are generally designated for a limited period of time with a remit to effect transformational change that may well be politically difficult for a local authority that is subject to annual or four-yearly elections. At the end of their term, they cease to exist, while the local authority inherits what they have developed, and indeed probably takes ownership of some of their assets. The areas where New Town Development Corporations were established in the immediate post-war era, and again in the 1960s, have generally benefited hugely from their legacy, even if they complained bitterly at the time about their designation. We should not be afraid to repeat the same use of special purpose vehicles to implement necessary large-scale development such as New Towns or Garden Cities, which will be required in certain areas if Britain is to remain a successful country capable of accommodating a growing population.

The model that I am advocating is not one in which government transfers powers and washes its hands of the outcome. Government should continue to exercise a strategic oversight of what is happening in all parts of the country and it has, in my view, a responsibility to ensure that national priorities are met. Where necessary, because either of special development needs or the abject failure of a sub-national authority (see Chapter Eight), government may have to intervene, but in doing so it must distinguish between exceptional intervention for a defined and strategic purpose as against persistent meddling and micro-management. The former may be necessary from time to time. The latter is always damaging to local confidence and performance. Indeed, wherever intervention is needed, the aim of government should be to ensure that at the end of the process the local or sub-national authority is stronger and better able to discharge its responsibilities efficiently in the future.

There is a tension at the heart of the devolution debate between autonomy and fairness. In a very unequal world, where different areas enjoy hugely differing economic, social and environmental advantages, it would be wholly wrong for every area to be left to sink or swim on its own. Central government does have a responsibility to ensure that its resource-allocation arrangements seek to compensate for the disadvantages suffered by the poorest areas and provide a real opportunity for those areas to improve their conditions and prospects. It is equally right for government to intervene through initiatives such as the designation of the Thames Gateway, or to promote a Northern Powerhouse to seek transformational change that will redress historic imbalances in the life chances of people living in different areas. This is not incompatible with greater devolution of powers and responsibility. There is a distinction between government exercising strategic oversight and doing so with due regard for fairer distribution of resources, on the one hand, and indiscriminate meddling and micro-management from the centre, on the other. Understanding and applying that distinction is crucial.

Turning to the national scene, we have repeatedly encountered illustrations in the preceding chapters of problems attributable to a high turnover of ministers and the baleful effects of a lack of continuity on the implementation of policy. This has been identified as a fundamental problem time and again in studies of policy failures.[2] What is extraordinary is the way the Westminster 'family' continues to accept this inherently inefficient practice as an unavoidable corollary of the democratic process. It isn't. There is absolutely no reason why ministers should not continue to hold office, providing they are doing the job properly, for the duration of a Parliament or longer. Indeed, high turnover rates are not universal. The contrast between the shortness of most ministerial appointments and the degree of longevity in others is very revealing. In the 20 years from 1995 to 2015 no fewer than 13 individuals held the post of Housing Minister, each one lasting on average just a year and a half. By contrast, there have been just four chancellors of the Exchequer over the same period, averaging five years each. Gordon Brown served 10 years in the post, George Osborne is looking to get close to that figure, and Ken Clarke in the 1990s served for over four years. Only Alastair Darling, whose tenure was cut short by the general election in 2010, was in post for less than three years. Of course, chancellors are higher up the pecking order than almost all other ministers. But if prime ministers have to respect their positions and allow them time to shape the country's economy, should not the same logic apply to other ministerial posts?

Given the fact that most ministers will not be experts in the subjects for which they are responsible because, under British constitutional arrangements, they have to be directly answerable to and therefore overwhelmingly drawn from the membership of the House of Commons, there is all the more reason for allowing them adequate time to get to know their area of policy responsibility. In this way they are far more likely, assuming they are diligent, to develop a reasonable understanding of the sectors they are overseeing, to meet the key players, to learn from their perspectives, to win their respect and to understand better the implications of proposed changes in policy and practice. As I have already stressed (Chapter One) one of the fundamental problems facing our democracy is the sense of alienation on the part of the electorate, who perceive politicians at Westminster as being remote from the rest of the population, operating on very different rules and behaving as though they were part of a separate caste. The ministerial 'merry-go-round' could not be a clearer illustration of how Westminster follows different behaviour patterns to the rest of the world. Bringing it more into line with what happens elsewhere would not just be a recipe for better government; it could also help to reverse a potentially dangerous rift between the governors and the governed. Looking back in time, it is interesting that the turnover of housing ministers was far less in the immediate post-war period. In the 15 years from 1945 to 1960 there were just four housing ministers. I make no suggestion of direct causal links, but it is notable that housing output was very much higher in that period when housing ministers could expect to remain in office for the duration of a Parliament, and did expect to be judged on their output, which can be properly assessed only over a period of years. It was also a period when politicians were generally held in much higher regard by the British public.

So, as a start we should be insisting that ministerial appointments should, as a rule, and subject to competence in office, last for at least one parliamentary term. Ideally, ministers should come to office with some prior knowledge of the sector, perhaps through shadowing the minister while in opposition, or working as a Parliamentary Private Secretary when in government, and should have had some involvement in the formulation of the policies they will be expected to implement. A stronger human resources focus in the Whips' Office would help such career development; but, given the vagaries of the political process, this is not always achievable. Irrespective of this, ministers should be judged on their performance in post and should expect promotion only on the strength of proven success, not by the happy accident of an annual reshuffle. Being moved sooner should normally follow only a failure to perform, leading to demotion or a return to the back benches.

Such an approach to the appointment of senior and middle managers would be regarded as so obvious in any other walk of life as to make a recommendation in a book superfluous. But most serving politicians at Westminster, when presented with this proposition, smile and say something like 'It's a nice idea but it will never happen'. Disregarding normal principles of good management is not a sound basis for good government, and the sooner we recognise this the better. Prime ministers have lots of other tools to maintain loyalty and effective political management without debasing the process of ministerial appointments by making them on criteria that have little to do with individuals' skills and experience (see Chapter One) and also making them subject to an annual reshuffle. If we really want to improve the performance of government, this would be a very sensible starting point.

One of the likely consequences of such a reform would be much greater care on the part of prospective and serving ministers in the development of policy. With the prospects of promotion depending on performance in office there would be a strong incentive to make sure that new policy proposals were practical, workable and likely to deliver successful outcomes. This is not to deny the importance of creative thinking in the pursuit of new solutions to perceived or real problems. This is fundamental to the political process. However, there is a world of difference between the development of new policy proposals and their successful implementation. Too often the focus in the policy-development process is on the political attractiveness of the proposal rather than its 'real world' impact. With insufficient attention given to the question 'How?' it is not surprising that the outcome often fails to deliver the promised benefits. As I have already argued (Chapter One), the perverse consequence has been to damage the reputation and credibility of politicians and the whole political process. Spin, not substance, has been the perceived priority of politicians. Reversing this perception is essential if we are to begin to rebuild public confidence in the democratic process. Both government and Parliament have crucial roles to play in delivering this change, through testing, scrutinising and challenging new policy proposals to ensure that they have been properly thought through, that they are proportionate and well targeted, that they are necessary and capable of successful implementation, that they have a good prospect of achieving their objectives and that they do not bring unwelcome and unforeseen consequences. While, in theory, current parliamentary procedures should achieve this outcome, in reality they fall short all too often.

In theory, the preparation of impact assessments for all new legislation should help to identify potential problems, allowing remedial or compensating measures to be put in place at an early stage. But the way the procedure currently operates does not guarantee this. Too often, it has the hallmark of a box-ticking exercise rather than a rigorous analysis of what in practice is likely to occur. This is hardly surprising when the assessments are prepared in the department that is advocating the proposal, and there is therefore a strong incentive for the civil servants to come up with findings that support, or at least do not seriously challenge, the political objectives of the department. Occasionally the impact assessment does provide powerful evidence that can be deployed to overcome political prejudice, as illustrated with the case for the mandatory installation of smoke and carbon monoxide alarms described in Chapter Ten. But the system does not work as effectively as it should. An obligation to obtain independent verification of the departmental or Treasury findings, as for example happens with the Office for Budget Responsibility examination of the government's financial projections, would be a useful discipline.

In addition, some relatively simple procedural reforms that have been suggested on many previous occasions by, for example, the Better Government Initiative,[3] would help to promote the necessary changes. These would include:

1. formalised standards for the preparation of all new legislation;
2. direct ministerial accountability to Parliament for ensuring compliance with those standards;

3. new legislation to be published in draft, except in exceptional circumstances, to allow thorough pre-legislative scrutiny;
4. obligations on government to report to Parliament on how it has amended its proposals in response to issues identified during the process of pre-legislative scrutiny, and in evidence sessions at the start of Public Bill proceedings;
5. strict limitations on the introduction of new clauses during the parliamentary passage of legislation;
6. an obligation on government to publish in draft all secondary legislation (Statutory Instruments) expected to be issued under powers contained in the Bill, in time for scrutiny by the Public Bill Committee.

While these may appear relatively arcane procedural changes to current arrangements for the preparation and scrutiny of parliamentary Bills, they would, I believe, have a profound impact on the quality of new legislation by making those responsible more accountable for the content of (and omissions from) their Bills, and by closing loopholes that currently allow government to short-circuit or evade proper scrutiny. As much as anything this would encourage Parliament to do well the job of scrutiny that is supposedly central to its role.

Just as important as improving the quality of legislation is ensuring effective implementation. The implications will vary enormously from one Bill to the next, depending on its scope, the number of different measures requiring implementation, the number of organisations involved in that process, the time-scale, budget and personnel requirements and a number of other variables. But whether we are talking about a complex, multifaceted piece of legislation or a small, single-purpose measure, problems can all too easily occur that frustrate the hopes and expectations of those who have drafted the legislation. Similarly, work programmes that do not require new legislative sanction can also go awry in the implementation phase. Examples have been highlighted in earlier chapters (see in particular the section on FireControl in Chapter Nine). There are many factors that contribute to failures during the implementation phase, a number of which have been highlighted earlier in this book. The absence of detailed ministerial oversight, whether because of a reshuffle and lack of interest on the part of a new minister, or simply because other pressing issues have diverted a minister's attention, can have a dire effect, not least when there may be uncertainty among those responsible for implementation as to whether the measure continues to command political priority (see the section on 'Sellers' Packs' in Chapter Five). Lack of clarity in the respective roles and responsibilities of the various parties involved in implementation, particularly where different tiers of government or complex partnerships are involved, can equally damage the prospect of a successful transition from policy into practice. The capability of the civil service to implement policy is another key factor that has been a subject of repeated debate over many decades. While there have been advances in some areas, and a greater understanding of the importance of project management expertise within the civil service, this is and will, I suspect, remain a live issue for some years to come. The marked 'downsizing' of many departments since 2010 has reduced capacity, and not just in the field of policy analysis. Too many departments are currently struggling to cope with the multiple pressures they face and will not find it easy to raise their game in the implementation of policy.

Against this background there are obvious gains to be made from a more rigorous analysis, at the time when policy is being developed, of all the elements that will need to be activated or deployed to ensure efficient implementation. A better understanding of what the likely impacts will be on all the players on the field, what resources will be available to them and how they are likely to respond to different potential challenges during the implementation phase would certainly help those responsible to plan ahead and cope with difficulties that might not have been foreseen when the policy was first evolved. This simply can't be outsourced to consultants. As we saw in relation to FireControl (Chapter Nine) excessive dependence on consultants in the absence of necessary skills within the civil service can have disastrous consequences. Reducing pressures on government through devolution, as advocated earlier, should certainly help to give the civil service more space to do its core job well, but if this is to deliver real improvements there will have to be sustained focus on ensuring the right mix of skills in

Whitehall, both to develop and to implement policy, and a clear understanding that these are not separate skills to be deployed in isolation. From the outset, good policy development requires a full understanding of what will be needed to ensure successful implementation.

I have already highlighted the inadequacy of current procedures for evaluating the impact of new legislation and new policy initiatives. This will certainly need to be addressed if we are to understand better why some measures worked and others didn't, as well as learn how to do better in future. Individual government departments and departmental select committees should be far more rigorous in their approach to post-legislative scrutiny and the evaluation of how particular policy initiatives worked out in practice. Parliament itself could help by insisting that time is made available for debates on the impact of different pieces of legislation and other policy initiatives. To counter the obvious temptations for the party whips to seek to focus such debates only on the failures of their opponents, there would need to be an agreed cross-party framework, possibly involving the chairs of the departmental select committees, for agreeing the programme of such debates. This should cover a range of measures, some of which would be recent initiatives, others of which could be more long-standing and therefore likely to be the responsibility of former governments of different political complexions. As I have already argued (see Chapter Two), such longer-term evaluations could be very useful in identifying whether (and, if so, how) changes might be made to accommodate unforeseen developments or wider changes in the context within which a particular piece of legislation operates. Currently we have a tendency to consign too many pieces of legislation to a box marked 'The Past' rather than to understand that policy is a constantly evolving process in which regular re-evaluation and adjustment is needed to take account of changes in the wider environment.

If the way that Parliament legislates leaves a lot of room for improvement, the same critique applies in spades to the process by which the Prime Minister is supposedly held to account. Prime Minister's Questions (PMQs) is by far and away the most visible face of government in the UK, and unquestionably shapes public perceptions of the work of government and Parliament. The spectacle of a rowdy bear-pit in which the country's leading politicians try to score points at each other's expense, with scant regard to objective truth or the normal courtesies of debate, does little to enhance the reputation of Parliament. In his book based on his time working closely with Tony Blair, Jonathan Powell gives perhaps the best explanation of why this unedifying spectacle survives:

> The session, which is watched on TV by about a million people does nothing for any Prime Minister's standing in the country. The public hate the Punch and Judy sight of politicians slagging each other off. It is, however, an essential tool for rallying your troops on the back benches. Their mood for the week is determined by the leader's performance.[4]

The survival of PMQs, which has few serious supporters, is dependent on two factors. The first is, as Powell suggests, its value in terms of party management. The second is the lack of a credible alternative. Any move to replace PMQs with a less adversarial format, in which the Prime Minister might answer serious questions, or indeed enter into a dialogue or proper debate, is immediately dismissed as letting the Prime Minister 'off the hook', as though the weekly Wednesday bear-pit was actually holding him to account. It isn't. Successful prime ministers rapidly learn the art of deflecting any potentially damaging question with a witty put-down, a glib half-truth or a blatant refusal to answer. Provided that they maintain their cool and their show of confidence, they have nothing to fear from the current format. They would have a great deal more to fear from a better-structured question-and-answer session in which follow-up questions were the norm and the presumption was in favour of full and accurate responses. But the difficulty of combining such enquiry after the truth with the theatrical element and the party-political knockabout that characterise PMQs is the main reason why we persist with the clearly unsatisfactory current arrangement. In consequence we are perversely trapped into perpetuating a process that few, if any, of its active participants believe has any real merit and that damages the reputation of Parliament as the symbol of our country's democracy. At some stage the nettle will need to be grasped, and PMQs consigned to the past, because so long as it continues to represent the public face and the style of Westminster politics it is difficult to see the reputation of Parliament recovering fully from its present malaise.

The measures covered in this book and the specific proposals for reform advocated in this concluding chapter are by no means a panacea for all the ills of our system of government.

These are many and varied and will require a huge range of different responses to put them right. However, I do believe that we would make a significant start on the route by adopting the agenda set out above to improve the process by which we try to translate policy into practice. At the very least we could begin to reverse the dangerous trend in public thinking that assumes that politicians are 'only in it for themselves' by demonstrating a clearer commitment to introducing and implementing policies that have been well thought through, that are less plagued with errors, mistakes and failures and that do bring genuine benefits to the public. It is probably fanciful to anticipate the publication of a successor volume to Crewe and King's *The Blunders of Our Governments* a few years down the line under the title *The Wonders of Our Governments*! But it is not a bad ambition to aim for such an outcome.

Notes

Preface

[1] Mullin, C. (2009) *A view from the foothills. The diaries of Chris Mullin*, London: Profile (and two other volumes).

Chapter One

[1] Shakespeare, W., *King Lear*, Act IV, scene 6.

[2] Oborne, P. (2007) *The triumph of the political class*, London: Simon and Schuster.

[3] Hansard Society (2016) *Audit of political engagement*, No 13, p 6.

[4] King A. and Crewe, I. (2013) *The blunders of our governments*, London: Oneworld Publications.

[5] See Powell, J. (2010) *The new Machiavelli: How to wield power in the modern world*, London: Bodley Head; King and Crewe, 2013.

[6] Evidence to the House of Commons Public Administration Select Committee, 23 October 2008, in *Good government: Eighth report of session 2008–09*, vol 2, p EV48.

[7] *Standards in public life: First report of the Committee on Standards in Public Life* (1995) London: HMSO.

[8] Marcus Aurelius, *Meditations*.

Chapter Two

[1] National Assistance Act 1948, Section 21 (1) (b).

[2] Greve, J., Page, D. and Greve, S. (1971) *Homelessness in London*, Edinburgh: Scottish Academic Press.

[3] Donnison, D. and Ungerson, C. (1982) *Housing policy*, London: Penguin, p 271.

[4] Ibid, p 266.

[5] Glastonbury, B. (1971) *Homeless near a thousand homes*, London: Allen & Unwin, p 106.

[6] See in particular Deakin, N. (ed) (1986) *Policy change in government: Three case studies*, RIPA; Donnison and Ungerson, 1982; and Crowson, N. (2013) 'Revisiting the 1977 Housing (Homeless Persons) Act: Westminster, Whitehall, and the homelessness lobby', *Twentieth Century British History*, vol 24, no 3, pp 424–47.

7   Cambridge Centre for Housing and Planning Research (CCHPR), *UK Housing Review 2015*, Cambridge: CCHPR, Table 19b.
8   CCHPR, *UK Housing Review 2014*, Cambridge: CCHPR, chapter 5, Commentary, p 71.

Chapter Three

1   Kemp, P.A. (1992) *Housing Benefit: An appraisal*, London: HMSO, p 5.
2   Raynsford, N. and McGurk, P. (1982) *The guide to Housing Benefit*, London: SHAC and Institute of Housing.
3   *The Times*, 20 January 1984.
4   NACAB (1984) *Housing Benefit: The cost to the claimant*, NACAB.
5   Quoted in Kemp, P.A. (1984) *The cost of chaos: A survey of the Housing Benefit scheme*, London: SHAC, p 37.
6   Housing Benefit Review Team (1985) *Housing Benefit Review. Report of the Review Team*, Cmnd 9520, London: HMSO.
7   Cambridge Centre for Housing and Planning Research (CCHPR) *UK Housing Review 2015*, Cambridge: CCHPR, Table 20a.
8   Department of the Environment, Transport and the Regions (2000) *Quality and choice; A decent home for all. The Housing Green Paper*, London: DETR.
9   IPPR (2014) *Benefits to bricks*, London: IPPR.

Chapter Four

1   See, for example, McDonald, N. and Whitehead, C. (2015) 'New estimates of housing requirements in England', Tomorrow Series paper 17, London: TCPA.
2   Gregory, J. (2009) *In the mix: Narrowing the gap between public and private housing*, London: Fabian Society, pp 17–19.
3   Ibid, p 21.
4   See in particular Young, M. and Willmott, P. (1957) *Family and kinship in East London*, London: Routledge and Kegan Paul.
5   See, for example, Cherry, A. and Hodkinson, R. (2009) 'Millennium Homes revisited', *Ingenia*, Issue 41, December, www.ingenia.org.uk/Ingenia/Articles/579.
6   Urban Task Force (1999) *Towards an urban renaissance*, London: HMSO.
7   DCLG, *Land use change statistics 2013 to 2014*, Table P211.
8   Planning Policy Guidance Note PPG3 (1998) *Housing*, 'Use of density in urban planning'.
9   DCLG Housing Statistics, Live Table 118, 'Annual net additional dwellings 2000-01 to 2010-11', statistics no longer updated.
10 Speech by Nick Herbert MP on Second Reading of Housing and Planning Bill, *Hansard*, 2 November 2015, col 762.
11 Raynsford, N. (2013) *The challenge of the housing crisis*, London: TCPA, p 7.
12 The Lyons Housing Review (2014) *Mobilising across the nation to build the homes our children need*, www.yourbritain.org.uk/uploads/editor/files/The_Lyons_Housing_Review_2.pdf.

[13]   Howard, E. (1898) *Tomorrow: A peaceful path to real reform*, London: Swan Sonnenschein.

Chapter Five

[1]   *Ending discrimination against disabled people* (1995) Cm 2729, London: HMSO.

[2]   DETR, *1998 review of Part L, Building Regulations* (1998).

[3]   DCLG (2007) *Building a greener future: Towards zero carbon development*, London: DCLG.

[4]   See Kippin, H., Hauf, H. and Shafique, A. (2012) *Business, society and public services, a social productivity framework*, London: RSA.

[5]   See BRE (2013) *Lessons from AIMC4 for cost-effective, fabric-first, low-energy housing*, Watford, BRE Publications.

[6]   See, for example, NHBC Foundation (2008) *Zero carbon: what does it mean to homeowners and housebuilders?* IHS BRE Press; NHBC Foundation (2012) *Today's attitudes to low and zero carbon homes*, IHS BRE Press.

[7]   Lord Chancellor's Department, Department of Trade and Industry and DETR (1998) *Key research on easier home buying and selling: Main report* (December).

[8]   Housing Act 2004, Part 5.

[9]   See, for example, Dorey, P. (2014) *Policy making in Britain*, 2nd edn, London: Sage Publications.

[10]   Lord, F. (ed) (2010) *The stabilization of Combe Down Stone Mines: the saving of a village*, HCA and Bath and North East Somerset Council.

[11]   BRE Information Bulletin (1998), DETR archive.

[12]   BRE Proposal to DETR for eradication programme, September 1998, DETR archive.

[13]   Ibid.

[14]   Ibid.

[15]   BRE Briefing note for DETR, July 1998, DETR archive.

Chapter Six

[1]   *New leadership for London: The government's proposals for a Greater London Authority* (1997) London: TSO (July).

[2]   *A mayor and assembly for London': The government's proposals for modernizing the governance of London* (1998) London: TSO (March).

[3]   Travers, T. (2013) *Raising the capital: The report of the London Finance Commission*, London: London Finance Commission.

[4]   Jenkins, S. (1998) *Evening Standard* (24 September).

Chapter Seven

[1]   Cabinet Office and DTLR (2002) *Your region, your choice. Revitalising the English regions*, Cm 5511, London: HMSO, Foreword.

[2]   Ibid, p 9.

3   The Electoral Commission (2005) *The 2004 North East regional assembly
    and local government referendums,* London: The Electoral Commission.
4   See, for example, Jenkins, S. (2001) 'Guess which of these men runs London',
    Evening Standard (21 June).
5   City Finance Commission (2011) *Setting cities free – releasing the potential of
    cities to drive growth. Final report of the City Finance Commission.*
6   Travers, T. (2013) *Raising the capital: The report of the London Finance
    Commission,* London: London Finance Commission
7   Parker, S. (2015) *Taking power back,* Bristol: Policy Press, p 63.

Chapter Eight
1   Hackney Council submission to Audit Commission, CPA self-assessment,
    July 2002.
2   Ibid.
3   'Hackney launches fraud probe', *Public Finance* (February), 16 February
    2001.
4   A. Klonowski, Acting Director of Finance and Performance, Hackney
    Council, note to DTLR, 22 February 2001.
5   *Observer,* 12 November 2000.
6   Audit Commission (2000) 'Best Value Inspection. London Borough of
    Hackney' (November), DETR archive.
7   IDeA (1999) Peer review of Hackney Council (November).
8   Private conversation with Max Caller.
9   Audit Commission (2003) London Borough of Hackney, annual audit letter
    (January).
10 ODPM (2006) submission to Jim Fitzpatrick MP (6 February).
11 See Burton, M. (2013) *The politics of public sector reform,* London:
    Macmillan, pp 156–8.
12 *Financial Times,* 9 January 2003, quoted in Campbell-Smith, D. (2008) *Follow
    the money: The Audit Commission, public money and the management of public
    services, 1983–2008,* London: Allen Lane, pp 529–30.
13 Burton, 2013, pp 158–9.
14 Campbell-Smith, 2008, p 573.

Chapter Nine
1   The Bain Report (2002) *The future of the Fire Service: reducing risk, saving
    lives. The independent review of the Fire Service,* London: TSO.
2   Ibid.
3   Ibid, Foreword.
4   See *Sunday Times,* 2 March 2003.
5   Private conversation with Denis (now Lord) Tunnicliffe, 1997.
6   Fire and Rescue Services Act 2004, London: TSO.
7   The Bain Report, 2002, para 7.40.

8   House of Commons Communities and Local Government Committee (2006) *Fire and Rescue Service. Fourth Report of Session 2005–06*, London: TSO, p 37.
9   Knight, K. (2013) *Facing the future: Findings from the review of efficiencies and operations in fire and rescue authorities in England*, London: DCLG, p 12.
10 Ibid, p 45.
11 ODPM, *Our Fire and Rescue Service*, Cm 5808, p 29.
12 Mott MacDonald (2000) *The future of Fire and Rescue Service control rooms in England and Wales*, updated 2003, ODPM archive.
13 National Audit Office (2011) *The failure of the FireControl project*, London: TSO.
14 OGC (2004) Healthcheck report on FireControl project (21 October) ODPM archive.
15 ODPM archive (December 2004)
16 The Smoke and Carbon Monoxide Alarm (England) Regulations 2015.

Chapter Ten

1   Hall, P. (1963) *London 2000*, London: Faber, 3rd edn 1971.
2   Abercrombie, L.P. and Forshaw, J.H. (1943) *County of London Plan 1943*, London: Macmillan and Company Ltd; Abercrombie, L.P. (1944) *Greater London Plan*, London: University of London Press.
3   *East Thames Corridor. A study of development capacity and potential* (1993) London: HMSO.
4   Department of the Environment (1995) *The Thames Gateway planning framework* (RPG9A), London: HMSO.
5   Wray, I. (2015) *Great British plans: Who made them and how they worked*, London: Routledge, chapter 9.
6   See Soulsby, Sir Peter, *Hansard*, 31 October 2006, cols 258–9.
7   Ibid, col 240.

Chapter Eleven

1   See Mulgan, G. and Bury, F. (eds) (2006) *Double devolution: The renewal of local government*, London: Sage Publications.
2   See, for example, King, A. and Crewe, I. (2013) *The blunders of our governments*, London: Oneworld Publications, chapter 22.
3   The Better Government Initiative (2010) 'Good government. Reforming Parliament and the executive', www.bettergovernmentinitiative.co.uk.
4   Powell, J. (2010) *The new Machiavelli: How to wield power in the modern world*, London: Bodley Head, p 159.

Index

Index

Rogers, Richard 60
Rooker, Jeff 87
Ross, Stephen 28
rough sleeping 29, 33, 35

S

Sandford, Jeremy 20
Saunton 92–5
Scotland
devolution 15, 97, 98, 99, 100,
111, 116
Fire and Rescue Service 156, 160
homelessness 34
house-buying and selling process
84
Labour Party 6
Section 106 agreements 62
sellers' packs 84–9, 186
SERPLAN 170
Shakespeare, William 1
Shelter 20, 23, 25
Shelter Housing Aid Centre
(SHAC) 19–20, 23
Shore, Peter 28
Shuttleworth, Ken 108
Silkin, Lewis 72–3
single homeless people 27–8, 29,
33, 34
SNP (Scottish National Party) 4, 5
social housing *see* council housing;
housing associations
Social Housing Grant 46
social media 12–14
Social Security Advisory
Committee (SSAC) 39, 42
Social Security and Housing Benefit
Act 1982 42
social segregation 55–6, 57, 72
South West 114, 115
Special Advisors (SPADs) 11
special purpose vehicles 169–70,
181, 182, 189–90
starter home scheme 68
Stratford 172, 173, 174, 176, 181,
182
Supplementary Benefit 38, 39

T

termites 92–5
terrorism 149
Thames Gateway 167–82, 189, 190
Thatcher, Margaret 97, 172
Timmins, Nick 139–40

Town and Country Planning Act
1947 73
transport
airports 180–1
Crossrail 175–9
Docklands Light Railway 175
Jubilee Line 104, 173–4
London Underground 104
regional devolution 103–4,
117–18
Thames Gateway 170–82
Transport for London (TfL) 103–4,
117, 118
Treasury
Channel Tunnel Rail Link 173
Crossrail 176–7, 178–9
London Underground 104
planning system 65, 66
Turnbull, Andrew 99–100
turnout 2, 3
Turton, Genie 101

U

UKIP (UK Independence Party) 5
Ungerson, C. 21–2
unitary local authorities 114,
115–16, 119–20, 150, 189
Urban Taskforce 60

V

Vadera, Shriti 179
voluntary organisations 24–5

W

Wales
Council Tax 9
devolution 15, 97, 98, 100, 111
Fire and Rescue Service 156
Wandsworth 142
Widdowson, Bob 23
Wilson, Des 20
Wolfson Prize 69–70
Wood, Philip 151
Woolwich 175, 176–9

Y

Yes, Minister 185
Young, Sir George 38
Young, Robin 101
Young, Sir Toby 152

Z

Zero Carbon 82